William Hazlitt

On the Pleasure of Hating

PENGUIN BOOKS — GREAT IDEAS

PENGUIN BOOKS

Published by the Penguin Group
Penguin Books Ltd, 80 Strand, London WC2R ORL, England
Penguin Group (USA) Inc., 375 Hudson Street, New York, New York 10014, USA
Penguin Books Australia Ltd, 250 Camberwell Road,
Camberwell, Victoria 3124, Australia
Penguin Books Canada Ltd, 10 Alcorn Avenue, Toronto, Ontario, Canada M4V 3B2
Penguin Books India (P) Ltd, 11 Community Centre,
Panchsheel Park, New Delhi – 110 017, India
Penguin Group (NZ), Cnr Airborne and Rosedale Roads,
Albany, Auckland 1310, New Zealand
Penguin Books (South Africa) (Pty) Ltd, 24 Sturdee Avenue,
Rosebank 2196, South Africa

Penguin Books Ltd, Registered Offices: 80 Strand, London WC2R ORL, England

www.penguin.com

This collection first published in Penguin Books 2004
9

Taken from the Penguin Classics editions *Selected Writings*,
edited by Ronald Blythe, and *The Fight and Other Writings*,
edited by Tom Paulin and David Chandler

Set in Monotype Dante
Typeset by Rowland Phototypesetting Ltd, Bury St Edmunds, Suffolk
Printed in England by Clays Ltd, St Ives plc

Contents

The Fight

'– The *fight*, the *fight's* the thing,
Wherein I'll catch the conscience of the king.'

Where there's a will, there's a way – I said to myself, as I walked down Chancery-lane, about half-past six o'clock on Monday the 10th of December, to inquire at Jack Randall's where the fight the next day was to be; and I found 'the proverb' nothing 'musty' in the present instance. I was determined to see this fight, come what would, and see it I did, in great style. It was my *first fight*, yet it more than answered my expectations. Ladies – it is to you I dedicate this description; nor let it seem out of character for the fair to notice the exploits of the brave. Courage and modesty are the old English virtues; and may they never look cold and askance on one another! Think, ye fairest of the fair, loveliest of the lovely kind, ye practisers of soft enchantment, how many more ye kill with poisoned baits than ever fell in the ring; and listen with subdued air and without shuddering, to a tale tragic only in appearance, and sacred to the FANCY!

I was going down Chancery-lane, thinking to ask at Jack Randall's where the fight was to be, when looking through the glass-door of the *Hole in the Wall*, I heard a

I

gentleman asking the same question *at* Mrs Randall, as the author of Waverley would express it. Now Mrs Randall stood answering the gentleman's question, with the authenticity of the lady of the Champion of the Light Weights. Thinks I, I'll wait till this person comes out, and learn from him how it is. For to say a truth, I was not fond of going into this house of call for heroes and philosophers, ever since the owner of it (for Jack is no gentleman) threatened once upon a time to kick me out of doors for wanting a mutton-chop at his hospitable board, when the conqueror in thirteen battles was more full of *blue ruin* than of good manners. I was the more mortified at this repulse, inasmuch as I had heard Mr James Simpkins, hosier in the Strand, one day when the character of the *Hole in the Wall* was brought in question, observe – 'The house is a very good house, and the company quite genteel: I have been there myself!' Remembering this unkind treatment of mine host, to which mine hostess was also a party, and not wishing to put her in unquiet thoughts at a time jubilant like the present, I waited at the door, when, who should issue forth but my friend Joe Toms, and turning suddenly up Chancery-lane with that quick jerk and impatient stride which distinguishes a lover of the FANCY, I said, 'I'll be hanged if that fellow is not going to the fight, and is on his way to get me to go with him.' So it proved in effect, and we agreed to adjourn to my lodgings to discuss measures with that cordiality which makes old friends like new, and new friends like old, on great occasions. We are cold to others only when we are dull in ourselves, and have neither thoughts nor feelings to impart to them. Give a man a topic in his head, a throb of pleasure in his heart, and he will be glad to share it with the first person he meets. Toms and I, though we seldom meet, were an *alter idem** on this memorable occasion, and had not an idea that we did not candidly impart; and 'so carelessly did we fleet the time,' that I wish no better, when there is another fight, than to have him for a companion on my journey down, and to return with my friend Jack Pigott talking of what was to happen or of what did happen, with a noble subject always at hand, and liberty to digress to others whenever they offered. Indeed, on my repeating the lines from Spenser in an involuntary fit of enthusiasm,

> 'What more felicity can fall to creature,
> Than to enjoy delight with liberty?'

my last-named ingenious friend stopped me by saying that this, translated into the vulgate, meant '*Going to see a fight.*'

Joe Toms and I could not settle about the method of going down. He said there was a caravan, he understood, to start from Tom Belcher's at two, which would go there *right out* and back again the next day. Now I never travel all night, and said I should get a cast to Newbury by one of the mails. Joe swore the thing was impossible, and I could only answer that I had made up my mind to it. In short, he seemed to me to waver, said he only came to see if I was going, had letters to write, a cause coming

---

* [each] another self.

on the day after, and faintly said at parting (for I was bent on setting out that moment) – 'Well, we meet at Philippi!' I made the best of my way to Piccadilly. The mail coach stand was bare. 'They are all gone,' said I – 'this is always the way with me – in the instant I lose the future – if I had not stayed to pour out that last cup of tea, I should have been just in time' – and cursing my folly and ill-luck together, without inquiring at the coach-office whether the mails were gone or not, I walked on in despite, and to punish my own dilatoriness and want of determination. At any rate, I would not turn back: I might get to Hounslow, or perhaps farther, to be on my road the next morning. I passed Hyde Park Corner (my Rubicon), and trusted to fortune. Suddenly I heard the clattering of a Brentford stage, and the fight rushed full upon my fancy. I argued (not unwisely) that even a Brentford coachman was better company than my own thoughts (such as they were just then), and at his invitation mounted the box with him. I immediately stated my case to him – namely, my quarrel with myself for missing the Bath or Bristol mail, and my determination to get on in consequence as well as I could, without any disparagement or insulting comparison between longer or shorter stages. It is a maxim with me that stage-coaches, and consequently stage-coachmen, are respectable in proportion to the distance they have to travel: so I said nothing on that subject to my Brentford friend. Any incipient tendency to an abstract proposition, or (as he might have construed it) to a personal reflection of this kind, was however nipped in the bud; for I had no sooner declared indignantly that I had missed the mails, than he flatly denied that they were gone along, and lo! at the instant three of them drove by in rapid, provoking, orderly succession, as if they would devour the ground before them. Here again I seemed in the contradictory situation of the man in Dryden who exclaims,

'I follow Fate, which does too hard pursue!'

If I had stopped to inquire at the White Horse Cellar, which would not have taken me a minute, I should now have been driving down the road in all the dignified unconcern and *ideal* perfection of mechanical convey-ance. The Bath mail I had set my mind upon, and I had missed it, as I missed every thing else, by my own absurdity, in putting the will for the deed, and aiming at ends without employing means. 'Sir,' said he of the Brentford, 'the Bath mail will be up presently, my brother-in-law drives it, and I will engage to stop him if there is a place empty.' I almost doubted my good genius; but, sure enough, up it drove like lightning, and stopped directly at the call of the Brentford Jehu. I would not have believed this possible, but the brother-in-law of a mail-coach driver is himself no mean man. I was trans-ferred without loss of time from the top of one coach to that of the other, desired the guard to pay my fare to the Brentford coachman for me as I had no change, was accommodated with a great coat, put up my umbrella to keep off a drizzling mist, and we began to cut through the air like an arrow. The mile-stones disappeared one after another, the rain kept off; Tom Turtle, the trainer, sat before me on the coach-box, with whom I exchanged civilities as a gentleman going to the fight; the passion that had transported me an hour before was subdued to pensive regret and conjectural musing on the next day's battle; I was promised a place inside at Reading, and upon the whole, I thought myself a lucky fellow. Such is the force of imagination! On the outside of any other coach on the 10th of December, with a Scotch mist drizzling through the cloudy moonlight air, I should have been cold, comfortless, impatient, and, no doubt, wet through; but seated on the Royal mail, I felt warm and comfortable, the air did me good, the ride did me good, I was pleased with the progress we had made, and confident that all would go well through the journey. When I got inside at Reading, I found Turtle and a stout valetudinarian, whose costume bespoke him one of the FANCY, and who had risen from a three months' sick bed to get into the mail to see the fight. They were intimate, and we fell into a lively discourse. My friend the trainer was confined in his topics to fighting dogs and men, to bears and badgers; beyond this he was 'quite chap-fallen,' had not a word to throw at a dog, or indeed very wisely fell asleep, when any other game was started. The whole art of training (I, however, learnt from him) consists in two things, exercise and abstinence, abstinence and exercise, repeated alternately and without end. A yolk of an egg with a spoonful of rum in it is the first thing in a morning, and then a walk of six miles till breakfast. This meal consists of a plentiful supply of tea and toast and beef-steaks. Then another six or seven miles till dinner-time, and another supply of solid beef or mutton with a pint of porter, and perhaps, at the utmost, a couple of glasses of sherry. Martin trains on water, but this increases his infirmity on another very dangerous side. The Gas-man takes now and then a chirping glass (under the rose) to console him, during a six weeks' probation, for the absence of Mrs Hickman – an agreeable woman, with (I understand) a pretty fortune of two hundred pounds. How matter presses on me! What stubborn things are facts! How inexhaustible is nature and art! 'It is well,' as I once heard Mr Richmond observe, 'to see a variety.' He was speaking of cock-fighting as an edifying spectacle. I cannot deny but that one learns more of what *is* (I do not say of what *ought to be*) in this desultory mode of practical study, than from reading the same book twice over, even though it should be a moral treatise. Where was I? I was sitting at dinner with the candidate for the honours of the ring, 'where good digestion waits on appetite, and health on both.' Then follows an hour of social chat and native glee; and afterwards, to another breathing over healthy hill or dale. Back to supper, and then to bed, and up by six again – Our hero

'Follows so the ever-running sun
With profitable *ardour*'–

to the day that brings him victory or defeat in the green fairy circle. Is not this life more sweet than mine? I was going to say; but I will not libel any life by comparing it to mine, which is (at the date of these presents) bitter as coloquintida and the dregs of aconitum!

The invalid in the Bath mail soared a pitch above the

trainer, and did not sleep so sound, because he had 'more figures and more fantasies.' We talked the hours away merrily. He had faith in surgery, for he had had three ribs set right, that had been broken in a *turn-up* at Belcher's, but thought physicians old women, for they had no antidote in their catalogue for brandy. An indigestion is an excellent common-place for two people that never met before. By way of ingratiating myself, I told him the story of my doctor, who, on my earnestly representing to him that I thought his regimen had done me harm, assured me that the whole pharmacopeia contained nothing comparable to the prescription he had given me; and, as a proof of its undoubted efficacy, said that, 'he had had one gentleman with my complaint under his hands for the last fifteen years.' This anecdote made my companion shake the rough sides of his three great coats with boisterous laughter; and Turtle, starting out of his sleep, swore he knew how the fight would go, for he had had a dream about it. Sure enough the rascal told us how the three first rounds went off, but 'his dream,' like others, 'denoted a foregone conclusion.' He knew his men. The moon now rose in silver state, and I ventured, with some hesitation, to point out this object of placid beauty, with the blue serene beyond, to the man of science, to which his ear he 'seriously inclined,' the more as it gave promise *d'un beau jour* for the morrow, and showed the ring undrenched by envious showers, arrayed in sunny smiles. Just then, all going on well, I thought on my friend Toms, whom I had left behind, and said innocently, 'There was a blockhead of a fellow I left in town, who said there was no possibility of getting down by the mail, and talked of going by a caravan from Belcher's at two in the morning, after he had written some letters.' 'Why,' said he of the lapells, 'I should not wonder if that was the very person we saw running about like mad from one coach-door to another, and asking if any one had seen a friend of his, a gentleman going to the fight, whom he had missed stupidly enough by staying to write a note.' 'Pray, Sir,' said my fellow-traveller, 'had he a plaid-cloak on?' – 'Why, no,' said I, 'not at the time I left him, but he very well might afterwards, for he offered to lend me one.' The plaid-cloak and the letter decided the thing. Joe, sure enough, was in the Bristol mail, which preceded us by about fifty yards. This was droll enough. We had now but a few miles to our place of destination, and the first thing I did on alighting at Newbury, both coaches stopping at the same time, was to call out, 'Pray, is there a gentleman in that mail of the name of Toms?' 'No,' said Joe, borrowing something of the vein of Gilpin, 'for I have just got out.' 'Well!' says he, 'this is lucky; but you don't know how vexed I was to miss you; for,' added he, lowering his voice, 'do you know when I left you I went to Belcher's to ask about the caravan, and Mrs Belcher said very obligingly she couldn't tell about that, but there were two gentlemen who had taken places by the mail and were gone on in a landau, and she could frank us. It's a pity I didn't meet with you; we could then have got down for nothing. But *mum's the word*.' It's the devil for any one to tell me a secret, for it's sure to come out in print. I do not care so much to gratify a friend, but the public ear is too great a temptation to me.

Our present business was to get beds and a supper at an inn; but this was no easy task. The public-houses were full, and where you saw a light at a private house, and people poking their heads out of the casement to see what was going on, they instantly put them in and shut the window, the moment you seemed advancing with a suspicious overture for accommodation. Our guard and coachman thundered away at the outer gate of the Crown for some time without effect – such was the greater noise within; – and when the doors were unbarred, and we got admittance, we found a party assembled in the kitchen round a good hospitable fire, some sleeping, others drinking, others talking on politics and on the fight. A tall English yeoman (something like Matthews in the face, and quite as great a wag) –

'A lusty man to ben an abbot able,' –

was making such a prodigious noise about rent and taxes, and the price of corn now and formerly, that he had prevented us from being heard at the gate. The first thing I heard him say was to a shuffling fellow who wanted to be off a bet for a shilling glass of brandy and water – 'Confound it, man, don't be *insipid*!' Thinks I, that is a good phrase. It was a good omen. He kept it up so all night, nor flinched with the approach of morning. He was a fine fellow, with sense, wit, and spirit, a hearty body and a joyous mind, free-spoken, frank, convivial – one of that true English breed that went with Harry the Fifth to the siege of Harfleur – 'standing like greyhounds in the slips,' &c. We ordered tea and eggs (beds were soon found to be out of the question) and this fellow's conversation was *sauce piquante*. It did one's heart good to see him brandish his oaken towel and to hear him talk. He made mince-meat of a drunken, stupid, red-faced, quarrelsome, *frowsy* farmer, whose nose 'he moralised into a thousand similes,' making it out a firebrand like Bardolph's. 'I'll tell you what, my friend,' says he, 'the landlady has only to keep you here to save fire and candle. If one was to touch your nose, it would go off like a piece of charcoal.' At this the other only grinned like an idiot, the sole variety in his purple face being his little peering eyes and yellow teeth; called for another glass, swore he would not stand it; and after many attempts to provoke his humorous antagonist to single combat, which the other turned off (after working him up to a ludicrous pitch of choler) with great adroitness, he fell quietly asleep with a glass of liquor in his hand, which he could not lift to his head. His laughing persecutor made a speech over him, and turning to the opposite side of the room, where they were all sleeping in the midst of this 'loud and furious fun,' said, 'There's a scene, by G—d, for Hogarth to paint. I think he and Shakespear were our two best men at copying life.' This confirmed me in my good opinion of him. Hogarth, Shakespear, and Nature, were just enough for him (indeed for any man) to know. I said, 'You read Cobbett, don't you? At least,' says I, 'you talk just as well as he writes.' He seemed to doubt this. But I said, 'We have an hour to spare: if you'll get pen, ink, and paper, and keep on talking, I'll write down what you say; and if it doesn't make a capital Political Register, I'll forfeit my head. You have kept me alive to-night, however. I don't know what I should have done without you.' He did not dislike this view of the thing, nor my asking if he was not about the size of Jem Belcher; and told me soon afterwards, in the confidence of friendship, that 'the circumstance which had given him nearly the greatest concern in his life, was Cribb's beating Jem after he had lost his eye by racket-playing.' – The morning dawns; that dim but yet clear light appears, which weighs like solid bars of metal on the sleepless eyelids; the guests drop down from their chambers one by one – but it was too late to think of going to bed now (the clock was on the stroke of seven), we had nothing for it but to find a barber's (the pole that glittered in the morning sun lighted us to his shop), and then a nine miles' march to Hungerford. The day was fine, the sky was blue, the mists were retiring from the marshy ground, the path was tolerably dry, the sitting-up all night had not done us much harm – at least the cause was good; we talked of this and that with amicable difference, roving and sipping of many subjects, but still invariably we returned to the fight. At length, a mile to the left of Hungerford, on a gentle eminence, we saw the ring surrounded by covered carts, gigs, and carriages, of which hundreds had passed us on the road; Toms gave a youthful shout, and we hastened down a narrow lane to the scene of action.

Reader, have you ever seen a fight? If not, you have a pleasure to come, at least if it is a fight like that between the Gas-man and Bill Neate. The crowd was very great when we arrived on the spot; open carriages were coming up, with streamers flying and music playing, and the country-people were pouring in over hedge and ditch in all directions, to see their hero beat or be beaten. The odds were still on Gas, but only about five to four. Gully had been down to try Neate, and had backed him considerably, which was a damper to the sanguine confidence of the adverse party. About two hundred thousand pounds were pending. The Gas says, he has lost 3000*l*. which were promised him by different gentlemen if he had won. He had presumed too much on himself, which had made others presume on him. This spirited and formidable young fellow seems to have taken for his motto the old maxim, that 'there are three things necessary to success in life – *Impudence! Impudence! Impudence!*' It is so in matters of opinion, but not in the FANCY, which is the most practical of all things, though even here confidence is half the battle, but only half. Our friend had vapoured and swaggered too much, as if he wanted to grin and bully his adversary out of the fight. 'Alas! the Bristol man was not so tamed!' – 'This is *the grave-digger*' (would Tom Hickman exclaim in the moments of intoxication from gin and success, shewing his tremendous right hand), 'this will send many of them to their long homes; I haven't done with them yet!' Why should he – though he had licked four of the best men within the hour, yet why should he threaten to inflict dishonourable chastisement on my old master Richmond, a veteran going off the stage, and who has borne his sable honours meekly? Magnanimity, my dear Tom, and bravery, should be inseparable. Or why should he go up to his antagonist, the first time he ever saw him at the Fives Court, and measuring him from head to foot with a glance of contempt, as Achilles surveyed Hector, say to him, 'What, are you Bill Neate? I'll knock more blood out of that great carcase of thine, this day fortnight, than you ever knock'd out of a bullock's!' It was not manly, 'twas not fighter-like. If he was sure of the victory (as he was not), the less said about it the better. Modesty should accompany the FANCY as its shadow. The best men were always the best behaved. Jem Belcher, the Game Chicken (before whom the Gas-man could not have lived) were civil, silent men. So is Cribb, so is Tom Belcher, the most elegant of sparrers, and not a man for every one to take by the nose. I enlarged on this topic in the mail (while Turtle was asleep), and said very wisely (as I thought) that impertinence was a part of no profession. A boxer was bound to beat his man, but not to thrust his fist, either actually or by implication, in every one's face. Even a highwayman, in the way of trade, may blow out your brains, but if he uses foul language at the same time, I should say he was no gentleman. A boxer, I would infer, need not be a blackguard or a coxcomb, more than another. Perhaps I press this point too much on a fallen man – Mr Thomas Hickman has by this time learnt that first of all lessons, 'That man was made to mourn.' He has lost nothing by the late fight but his presumption; and that every man may do as well without! By an over-display of this quality, however, the public had been prejudiced against him, and the *knowing-ones* were taken in. Few but those who had bet on him wished Gas to win. With my own prepossessions on the subject, the result of the 11th of

December appeared to me as fine a piece of poetical justice as I had ever witnessed. The difference of weight between the two combatants (14 stone to 12) was nothing to the sporting men. Great, heavy, clumsy, long-armed Bill Neate kicked the beam in the scale of the Gas-man's vanity. The amateurs were frightened at his big words, and thought that they would make up for the difference of six feet and five feet nine. Truly, the FANCY are not men of imagination. They judge of what has been, and cannot conceive of any thing that is to be. The Gas-man had won hitherto, therefore he must beat a man half as big again as himself – and that to a certainty. Besides, there are as many feuds, factions, prejudices, pedantic notions in the FANCY as in the state or in the schools. Mr Gully is almost the only cool, sensible man among them, who exercises an unbiassed discretion, and is not a slave to his passions in these matters. But enough of reflections, and to our tale. The day, as I have said, was fine for a December morning. The grass was wet, and the ground miry, and ploughed up with multitudinous feet, except that, within the ring itself, there was a spot of virgin-green closed in and unprofaned by vulgar tread, that shone with dazzling brightness in the mid-day sun. For it was now noon, and we had an hour to wait. This is the trying time. It is then the heart sickens, as you think what the two champions are about, and how short a time will determine their fate. After the first blow is struck, there is no opportunity for nervous apprehensions; you are swallowed up in the immediate interest of the scene – but

'Between the acting of a dreadful thing
And the first motion, all the interim is
Like a phantasma, or a hideous dream.'

I found it so as I felt the sun's rays clinging to my back, and saw the white wintry clouds sink below the verge of the horizon. 'So,' I thought, 'my fairest hopes have faded from my sight! – so will the Gas-man's glory, or that of his adversary, vanish in an hour.' The *swells* were parading in their white box-coats, the outer ring was cleared with some bruises on the heads and shins of the rustic assembly (for the *cockneys* had been distanced by the sixty-six miles); the time drew near, I had got a good stand; a bustle, a buzz, ran through the crowd, and from the opposite side entered Neate, between his second and bottle-holder. He rolled along, swathed in his loose great coat, his knock-knees bending under his huge bulk; and, with a modest cheerful air, threw his hat into the ring. He then just looked round, and began quietly to undress; when from the other side there was a similar rush and an opening made, and the Gas-man came forward with a conscious air of anticipated triumph, too much like the cock-of-the-walk. He strutted about more than became a hero, sucked oranges with a supercilious air, and threw away the skin with a toss of his head, and went up and looked at Neate, which was an act of supererogation. The only sensible thing he did was, as he strode away from the modern Ajax, to fling out his arms, as if he wanted to try whether they would do their work that day. By this time they had stripped, and presented a strong contrast in appearance. If Neate was like Ajax,

'with Atlantean shoulders, fit to bear' the pugilistic reputation of all Bristol, Hickman might be compared to
Diomed, light, vigorous, elastic, and his back glistened
in the sun, as he moved about, like a panther's hide.
There was now a dead pause – attention was awe-struck.
Who at that moment, big with a great event, did not
draw his breath short – did not feel his heart throb? All
was ready. They tossed up for the sun, and the Gas-man
won. They were led up to the *scratch* – shook hands, and
went at it.

In the first round every one thought it was all over.
After making play a short time, the Gas-man flew at his
adversary like a tiger, struck five blows in as many
seconds, three first, and then following him as he stag-
gered back, two more, right and left, and down he fell,
a mighty ruin. There was a shout, and I said, 'There is
no standing this.' Neate seemed like a lifeless lump of
flesh and bone, round which the Gas-man's blows played
with the rapidity of electricity or lightning, and you
imagined he would only be lifted up to be knocked down
again. It was as if Hickman held a sword or a fire in that
right hand of his, and directed it against an unarmed
body. They met again, and Neate seemed, not cowed,
but particularly cautious. I saw his teeth clenched
together and his brows knit close against the sun. He
held out both his arms at full length straight before him,
like two sledge-hammers, and raised his left an inch or
two higher. The Gas-man could not get over this guard
– they struck mutually and fell, but without advantage
on either side. It was the same in the next round; but the
balance of power was thus restored – the fate of the

battle was suspended. No one could tell how it would end. This was the only moment in which opinion was divided; for, in the next, the Gas-man aiming a mortal blow at his adversary's neck, with his right hand, and failing from the length he had to reach, the other returned it with his left at full swing, planted a tremendous blow on his cheek-bone and eyebrow, and made a red ruin of that side of his face. The Gas-man went down, and there was another shout – a roar of triumph as the waves of fortune rolled tumultuously from side to side. This was a settler. Hickman got up, and 'grinned horrible a ghastly smile,' yet he was evidently dashed in his opinion of himself; it was the first time he had ever been so punished; all one side of his face was perfect scarlet, and his right eye was closed in dingy blackness, as he advanced to the fight, less confident, but still determined. After one or two rounds, not receiving another such remembrancer, he rallied and went at it with his former impetuosity. But in vain. His strength had been weakened, – his blows could not tell at such a distance, – he was obliged to fling himself at his adversary, and could not strike from his feet; and almost as regularly as he flew at him with his right hand, Neate warded the blow, or drew back out of its reach, and felled him with the return of his left. There was little cautious sparring – no half-hits – no tapping and trifling, none of the *petit-maîtreship* of the art – they were almost all knock-down blows: – the fight was a good stand up fight. The wonder was the half-minute time. If there had been a minute or more allowed between each round, it would have been intelligible how they should by degrees recover strength and resolution; but to see two men smashed to the ground, smeared with gore, stunned, senseless, the breath beaten out of their bodies; and then, before you recover from the shock, to see them rise up with new strength and courage, stand steady to inflict or receive mortal offence, and rush upon each other 'like two clouds over the Caspian' – this is the most astonishing thing of all: – this is the high and heroic state of man! From this time forward the event became more certain every round; and about the twelfth it seemed as if it must have been over. Hickman generally stood with his back to me; but in the scuffle, he had changed positions, and Neate just then made a tremendous lunge at him, and hit him full in the face. It was doubtful whether he would fall backwards or forwards; he hung suspended for a second or two, and then fell back, throwing his hands in the air, and with his face lifted up to the sky. I never saw any thing more terrific than his aspect just before he fell. All traces of life, of natural expression, were gone from him. His face was like a human skull, a death's head, spouting blood. The eyes were filled with blood, the nose streamed with blood, the mouth gaped blood. He was not like an actual man, but like a preter-natural, spectral appearance, or like one of the figures in Dante's *Inferno*. Yet he fought on after this for several rounds, still striking the first desperate blow, and Neate standing on the defensive, and using the same cautious guard to the last, as if he had still all his work to do; and it was not till the Gas-man was so stunned in the seventeenth or eighteenth round, that his senses forsook him, and he could not come to time, that the battle was declared over.* Ye who despise the FANCY, do something to shew as much *pluck*, or as much self-possession as this, before you assume a superiority which you have never given a single proof of by any one action in the whole course of your lives! – When the Gas-man came to himself, the first words he uttered were, 'Where am I? What is the matter?' 'Nothing is the matter, Tom – you have lost the battle, but you are the bravest man alive.' And Jackson whispered to him, 'I am collecting a purse for you, Tom.' – Vain sounds, and unheard at that moment! Neate instantly went up and shook him cordially by the hand, and seeing some old acquaintance, began to flourish with his fists, calling out, 'Ah, you always said I couldn't fight – What do you think now?' But all in good-humour, and without any appearance of arrogance; only it was evident Bill Neate was pleased that he had won the fight. When it was over, I asked Cribb if he did not think it was a good one? He said, '*Pretty well!*' The carrier-pigeons now mounted into the air, and one of them flew with the news of her husband's victory to the bosom of Mrs Neate. Alas, for Mrs Hickman!

Mais au revoir, as Sir Fopling Flutter says. I went down

* Scroggins said of the Gas-man, that he thought he was a man of that courage, that if his hands were cut off, he would still fight on with the stumps – like that of Widrington, –

> – 'In doleful dumps,
> Who, when his legs were smitten off
> Still fought upon his stumps.'

with Toms; I returned with Jack Pigott, whom I met on the ground. Toms is a rattle-brain; Pigott is a sentimentalist. Now, under favour, I am a sentimentalist too – therefore I say nothing, but that the interest of the excursion did not flag as I came back. Pigott and I marched along the causeway leading from Hungerford to Newbury, now observing the effect of a brilliant sun on the tawny meads or moss-coloured cottages, now exulting in the fight, now digressing to some topic of general and elegant literature. My friend was dressed in character for the occasion, or like one of the FANCY; that is, with a double portion of great coats, clogs, and overhauls: and just as we had agreed with a couple of country-lads to carry his superfluous wearing-apparel to the next town, we were overtaken by a return post-chaise, into which I got, Pigott preferring a seat on the bar. There were two strangers already in the chaise, and on their observing they supposed I had been to the fight, I said I had, and concluded they had done the same. They appeared, however, a little shy and sore on the subject; and it was not till after several hints dropped, and questions put, that it turned out that they had missed it. One of these friends had undertaken to drive the other there in his gig: they had set out, to make sure work, the day before at three in the afternoon. The owner of the one-horse vehicle scorned to ask his way, and drove right on to Bagshot, instead of turning off at Hounslow: there they stopped all night, and set off the next day across the country to Reading, from whence they took coach, and got down within a mile or two of Hungerford, just half an hour after the fight was over. This might be safely set

down as one of the miseries of human life. We parted
with these two gentlemen who had been to see the fight,
but had returned as they went, at Wolhampton, where
we were promised beds (an irresistible temptation, for
Pigott had passed the preceding night at Hungerford as
we had done at Newbury), and we turned into an old
bow-windowed parlour with a carpet and a snug fire;
and after devouring a quantity of tea, toast, and eggs, sat
down to consider, during an hour of philosophic leisure,
what we should have for supper. In the midst of an
Epicurean deliberation between a roasted fowl and mutton chops with mashed potatoes, we were interrupted
by an inroad of Goths and Vandals – *O procul este profani**
– not real flash-men, but interlopers, noisy pretenders,
butchers from Tothill-fields, brokers from Whitechapel,
who called immediately for pipes and tobacco, hoping it
would not be disagreeable to the gentlemen, and began
to insist that it was *a cross*. Pigott withdrew from the
smoke and noise into another room, and left me to
dispute the point with them for a couple of hours *sans
intermission* by the dial. The next morning we rose
refreshed; and on observing that Jack had a pocket volume in his hand, in which he read in the intervals of our
discourse, I inquired what it was, and learned to my
particular satisfaction that it was a volume of the New
Eloise. Ladies, after this, will you contend that a love
for the FANCY is incompatible with the cultivation of
sentiment? – We jogged on as before, my friend setting
me up in a genteel drab great coat and green silk handker-

* You who are profane, stand at a distance.

chief (which I must say became me exceedingly), and after stretching our legs for a few miles, and seeing Jack Randall, Ned Turner, and Scroggins, pass on the top of one of the Bath coaches, we engaged with the driver of the second to take us to London for the usual fee. I got inside, and found three other passengers. One of them was an old gentleman with an aquiline nose, powdered hair, and a pigtail, and who looked as if he had played many a rubber at the Bath rooms. I said to myself, he is very like Mr Windham; I wish he would enter into conversation, that I might hear what fine observations would come from those finely-turned features. However, nothing passed, till, stopping to dine at Reading, some inquiry was made by the company about the fight, and I gave (as the reader may believe) an eloquent and animated description of it. When we got into the coach again, the old gentleman, after a graceful exordium, said, he had, when a boy, been to a fight between the famous Broughton and George Stevenson, who was called the *Fighting Coachman*, in the year 1770, with the late Mr Windham. This beginning flattered the spirit of prophecy within me and rivetted my attention. He went on –
'George Stevenson was coachman to a friend of my father's. He was an old man when I saw him some years afterwards. He took hold of his own arm and said, "there was muscle here once, but now it is no more than this young gentleman's." He added, "Well, no matter; I have been here long, I am willing to go hence, and I hope I have done no more harm than another man." Once,' said my unknown companion, 'I asked him if he had ever beat Broughton? He said Yes; that he had fought

23

with him three times, and the last time he fairly beat him, though the world did not allow it. "I'll tell you how it was, master. When the seconds lifted us up in the last round, we were so exhausted that neither of us could stand, and we fell upon one another, and as Master Broughton fell uppermost, the mob gave it in his favour, and he was said to have won the battle. But," says he; "the fact was, that as his second (John Cuthbert) lifted him up, he said to him, 'I'll fight no more, I've had enough;' which," says Stevenson, "you know gave me the victory. And to prove to you that this was the case, when John Cuthbert was on his death-bed, and they asked him if there was any thing on his mind which he wished to confess, he answered, 'Yes, that there was one thing he wished to set right, for that certainly Master Stevenson won that last fight with Master Broughton; for he whispered him as he lifted him up in the last round of all, that he had had enough'"' 'This,' said the Bath gentleman, 'was a bit of human nature;' and I have written this account of the fight on purpose that it might not be lost to the world. He also stated as a proof of the candour of mind in this class of men, that Stevenson acknowledged that Broughton could have beat him in his best day; but that he (Broughton) was getting old in their last rencounter. When we stopped in Piccadilly, I wanted to ask the gentleman some questions about the late Mr Windham, but had not courage. I got out, resigned my coat and green silk handkerchief to Pigott (loth to part with these ornaments of life), and walked home in high spirits.

P.S. Toms called upon me the next day, to ask me if I

did not think the fight was a complete thing? I said I thought it was. I hope he will relish my account of it.

From *The New Monthly Magazine* (February 1822), reprinted by Hazlitt's son in *Literary Remains* (1836).

The Indian Jugglers

COMING forward and seating himself on the ground in his white dress and tightened turban, the chief of the Indian Jugglers begins with tossing up two brass balls, which is what any of us could do, and concludes with keeping up four at the same time, which is what none of us could do to save our lives, nor if we were to take our whole lives to do it in. Is it then a trifling power we see at work, or is it not something next to miraculous? It is the utmost stretch of human ingenuity, which nothing but the bending the faculties of body and mind to it from the tenderest infancy with incessant, ever-anxious application up to manhood, can accomplish or make even a slight approach to. Man, thou art a wonderful animal, and thy ways past finding out! Thou canst do strange things, but thou turnest them to little account! – To conceive of this effort of extraordinary dexterity distracts the imagination and makes admiration breathless. Yet it costs nothing to the performer, any more than if it were a mere mechanical deception with which he had nothing to do but to watch and laugh at the astonishment of the spectators. A single error of a hair's-breadth, of the smallest conceivable portion of time, would be fatal: the precision of the movements must be like a mathematical truth, their rapidity is like lightning. To catch four balls in succession in less than a second of time, and deliver them back so as to return with seeming consciousness to the hand again, to make them revolve round him at certain intervals, like the planets in their spheres, to make them chase one another like sparkles of fire, or shoot up like flowers or meteors, to throw them behind his back and twine them round his neck like ribbons or like serpents, to do what appears an impossibility, and to do it with all the ease, the grace, the carelessness imaginable, to laugh at, to play with the glittering mockeries, to follow them with his eye as if he could fascinate them with its lambent fire, or as if he had only to see that they kept time with the music on the stage – there is something in all this which he who does not admire may be quite sure he never really admired any thing in the whole course of his life. It is skill surmounting difficulty, and beauty triumphing over skill. It seems as if the difficulty once mastered naturally resolved itself into ease and grace, and as if to be overcome at all, it must be overcome without an effort. The smallest awkwardness or want of pliancy or self-possession would stop the whole process. It is the work of witchcraft, and yet sport for children. Some of the other feats are quite as curious and wonderful, such as the balancing the artificial tree and shooting a bird from each branch through a quill; though none of them have the elegance or facility of the keeping up of the brass balls. You are in pain for the result, and glad when the experiment is over; they are not accompanied with the same unmixed, unchecked delight as the former; and I would not give much to be merely astonished without being pleased at the same time. As to the swallowing of the sword, the police ought to interfere to prevent it. When I saw the Indian Juggler do the same things before, his feet were bare, and he had large rings on the toes, which keep turning round all the time of the performance, as if they moved of themselves. – The hearing a speech in Parliament, drawled or stammered out by the Honourable Member or the Noble Lord, the ringing the changes on their common-places, which any one could repeat after them as well as they, stirs me not a jot, shakes not my good opinion of myself: but the seeing the Indian Juggler does. It makes me ashamed of myself. I ask what there is that I can do as well as this? Nothing. What have I been doing all my life? Have I been idle, or have I nothing to shew for all my labour and pains? Or have I passed my time in pouring words like water into empty sieves, rolling a stone up a hill and then down again, trying to prove an argument in the teeth of facts, and looking for causes in the dark, and not finding them? Is there no one thing in which I can challenge competition, that I can bring as an instance of exact perfection, in which others cannot find a flaw? The utmost I can pretend to is to write a description of what this fellow can do. I can write a book: so can many others who have not even learned to spell. What abortions are these Essays! What errors, what ill-pieced transitions, what crooked reasons, what lame conclusions! How little is made out, and that little how ill! Yet they are the best I can do. I endeavour to recollect all I have ever observed or thought upon a subject, and to express it as nearly as I can. Instead of writing on four subjects at a time, it is as much as I can manage to keep the thread of one discourse clear and unentangled. I have also time on my hands to correct my opinions, and polish my periods: but the one I cannot, and the other I will not do. I am fond of arguing: yet with a good deal of pains and practice it is often as much as I can do to beat my man; though he may be a very indifferent hand. A common fencer would disarm his adversary in the twinkling of an eye, unless he were a professor like himself. A stroke of wit will sometimes produce this effect, but there is no such power or superiority in sense or reasoning. There is no complete mastery of execution to be shewn there: and you hardly know the professor from the impudent pretender or the mere clown.*

I have always had this feeling of the inefficacy and slow progress of intellectual compared to mechanical excellence, and it has always made me somewhat dissatisfied. It is a great many years since I saw Richer, the famous rope-dancer, perform at Sadler's Wells. He was matchless in his art, and added to his extraordinary skill exquisite ease, and unaffected natural grace. I was at that

---

* The celebrated Peter Pindar (Dr Wolcot) first discovered and brought out the talents of the late Mr Opie, the painter. He was a poor Cornish boy, and was out at work in the fields, when the poet went in search of him. 'Well, my lad, can you go and bring me your very best picture?' The other flew like lightning, and soon came back with what he considered as his master-piece. The stranger looked at it, and the young artist, after waiting for some time without his giving any opinion, at length exclaimed eagerly, 'Well, what do you think of it?' – 'Think of it?' said Wolcot, 'why I think you ought to be ashamed of it – that you who might do so well, do no better!' The same answer would have applied to this artist's latest performances, that had been suggested by one of his earliest efforts.

time employed in copying a half-length picture of Sir Joshua Reynolds's; and it put me out of conceit with it. How ill this part was made out in the drawing! How heavy, how slovenly this other was painted! I could not help saying to myself, 'If the rope-dancer had performed his task in this manner, leaving so many gaps and botches in his work, he would have broke his neck long ago; I should never have seen that vigorous elasticity of nerve and precision of movement!' – Is it then so easy an undertaking (comparatively) to dance on a tightrope? Let any one, who thinks so, get up and try. There is the thing. It is that which at first we cannot do at all, which in the end is done to such perfection. To account for this in some degree, I might observe that mechanical dexterity is confined to doing some one particular thing, which you can repeat as often as you please, in which you know whether you succeed or fail, and where the point of perfection consists in succeeding in a given undertaking. – In mechanical efforts, you improve by perpetual practice, and you do so infallibly, because the object to be attained is not a matter of taste or fancy or opinion, but of actual experiment, in which you must either do the thing or not do it. If a man is put to aim at a mark with a bow and arrow, he must hit it or miss it, that's certain. He cannot deceive himself, and go on shooting wide or falling short, and still fancy that he is making progress. The distinction between right and wrong, between true and false, is here palpable; and he must either correct his aim or persevere in his error with his eyes open, for which there is neither excuse nor temptation. If a man is learning to dance on a rope, if he does not mind what he is about, he will break his neck. After that, it will be in vain for him to argue that he did not make a false step. His situation is not like that of Goldsmith's pedagogue.–

> 'In argument they own'd his wondrous skill,
> And e'en though vanquish'd, he could argue still.'

Danger is a good teacher, and makes apt scholars. So are disgrace, defeat, exposure to immediate scorn and laughter. There is no opportunity in such cases for self-delusion, no idling time away, no being off your guard (or you must take the consequences) – neither is there any room for humour or caprice or prejudice. If the Indian Juggler were to play tricks in throwing up the three case-knives, which keep their positions like the leaves of a crocus in the air, he would cut his fingers. I can make a very bad antithesis without cutting my fingers. The tact of style is more ambiguous than that of double-edged instruments. If the Juggler were told that by flinging himself under the wheels of the Jaggernaut, when the idol issues forth on a gaudy day, he would immediately be transported into Paradise, he might believe it, and nobody could disprove it. So the Brahmins may say what they please on that subject, may build up dogmas and mysteries without end, and not be detected: but their ingenious countryman cannot persuade the frequenters of the Olympic Theatre that he performs a number of astonishing feats without actually giving proofs of what he says. – There is then in this sort of manual dexterity, first a gradual aptitude acquired to a given exertion of muscular power, from constant repetition, and in the next place, an exact knowledge how much is still wanting and necessary to be supplied. The obvious test is to increase the effort or nicety of the operation, and still to find it come true. The muscles ply instinctively to the dictates of habit. Certain movements and impressions of the hand and eye, having been repeated together an infinite number of times, are unconsciously but unavoidably cemented into closer and closer union; the limbs require little more than to be put in motion for them to follow a regular track with ease and certainty; so that the mere intention of the will acts mathematically, like touching the spring of a machine, and you come with Locksley in Ivanhoe, in shooting at a mark, 'to allow for the wind.'

Farther, what is meant by perfection in mechanical exercises is the performing certain feats to a uniform nicety, that is, in fact, undertaking no more than you can perform. You task yourself, the limit you fix is optional, and no more than human industry and skill can attain to: but you have no abstract, independent standard of difficulty or excellence (other than the extent of your own powers). Thus he who can keep up four brass balls does this *to perfection*; but he cannot keep up five at the same instant, and would fail every time he attempted it. That is, the mechanical performer undertakes to emulate himself, not to equal another.* But the artist undertakes to imitate another, or to do what nature has done, and

---

* If two persons play against each other at any game, one of them necessarily fails.

this it appears is more difficult, *viz.* to copy what she has set before us in the face of nature or 'human face divine,' entire and without a blemish, than to keep up four brass balls at the same instant; for the one is done by the power of human skill and industry, and the other never was nor will be. Upon the whole, therefore, I have more respect for Reynolds, than I have for Richer: for, happen how it will, there have been more people in the world who could dance on a rope like the one than who could paint like Sir Joshua. The latter was but a bungler in his profession to the other, it is true; but then he had a harder task-master to obey, whose will was more wayward and obscure, and whose instructions it was more difficult to practise. You can put a child apprentice to a tumbler or rope-dancer with a comfortable prospect of success, if they are but sound of wind and limb: but you cannot do the same thing in painting. The odds are a million to one. You may make indeed as many H—s and H—s, as you put into that sort of machine, but not one Reynolds amongst them all, with his grace, his grandeur, his blandness of *gusto*, 'in tones and gestures hit,' unless you could make the man over again. To snatch this grace beyond the reach of art is then the height of art — where fine art begins, and where mechanical skill ends. The soft suffusion of the soul, the speechless breathing eloquence, the looks 'commercing with the skies,' the ever-shifting forms of an eternal principle, that which is seen but for a moment, but dwells in the heart always, and is only seized as it passes by strong and secret sympathy, must be taught by nature and genius, not by rules or study. It is suggested by feeling, not by laborious microscopic inspection: in seeking for it without, we lose the harmonious clue to it within: and in aiming to grasp the substance, we let the very spirit of art evaporate. In a word, the objects of fine art are not the objects of sight but as these last are the objects of taste and imagination, that is, as they appeal to the sense of beauty, of pleasure, and of power in the human breast, and are explained by that finer sense, and revealed in their inner structure to the eye in return. Nature is also a language. Objects, like words, have a meaning; and the true artist is the interpreter of this language, which he can only do by knowing its application to a thousand other objects in a thousand other situations. Thus the eye is too blind a guide of itself to distinguish between the warm or cold tone of a deep blue sky, but another sense acts as a monitor to it, and does not err. The colour of the leaves in autumn would be nothing without the feeling that accompanies it; but it is that feeling that stamps them on the canvas, faded, seared, blighted, shrinking from the winter's flaw, and makes the sight as true as touch—

> 'And visions, as poetic eyes avow,
> Cling to each leaf and hang on every bough.'

The more ethereal, evanescent, more refined and sublime part of art is the seeing nature through the medium of sentiment and passion, as each object is a symbol of the affections and a link in the chain of our endless being. But the unravelling this mysterious web of thought and feeling is alone in the Muse's gift, namely, in the power of that trembling sensibility which is awake to every change and every modification of its ever-varying impressions, that,

> 'Thrills in each nerve, and lives along the line.'

This power is indifferently called genius, imagination, feeling, taste; but the manner in which it acts upon the mind can neither be defined by abstract rules, as is the case in science, nor verified by continual unvarying experiments, as is the case in mechanical performances. The mechanical excellence of the Dutch painters in colouring and handling is that which comes the nearest in fine art to the perfection of certain manual exhibitions of skill. The truth of the effect and the facility with which it is produced are equally admirable. Up to a certain point, every thing is faultless. The hand and eye have done their part. There is only a want of taste and genius. It is after we enter upon that enchanted ground that the human mind begins to droop and flag as in a strange road, or in a thick mist, benighted and making little way with many attempts and many failures, and that the best of us only escape with half a triumph. The undefined and the imaginary are the regions that we must pass like Satan, difficult and doubtful, 'half flying, half on foot.' The object in sense is a positive thing, and execution comes with practice.

Cleverness is a certain *knack* or aptitude at doing certain things, which depend more on a particular adroitness and off-hand readiness than on force or perseverance, such as making puns, making epigrams, making extempore verses, mimicking the company, mimicking a style, &c. Cleverness is either liveliness and smartness, or something answering to *sleight of hand*, like letting a glass fall sideways off a table, or else a trick, like knowing the secret spring of a watch. Accomplishments are certain external graces, which are to be learnt from others, and which are easily displayed to the admiration of the beholder, *viz.* dancing, riding, fencing, music, and so on. These ornamental acquirements are only proper to those who are at ease in mind and fortune. I know an individual who if he had been born to an estate of five thousand a year, would have been the most accomplished gentleman of the age. He would have been the delight and envy of the circle in which he moved – would have graced by his manners the liberality flowing from the openness of his heart, would have laughed with the women, have argued with the men, have said good things and written agreeable ones, have taken a hand at piquet or the lead at the harpsichord, and have set and sung his own verses – *nugae canorae** – with tenderness and spirit; a Rochester without the vice, a modern Surrey! As it is, all these capabilities of excellence stand in his way. He is too versatile for a professional man, not dull enough for a political drudge, too gay to be happy, too thoughtless to be rich. He wants the enthusiasm of the poet, the severity of the prose-writer, and the application of the man of business. – Talent is the capacity of doing any thing that depends on application and industry, such as writing a criticism, making a speech, studying the law. Talent differs from genius, as voluntary differs from

* Trifling songs.

involuntary power. Ingenuity is genius in trifles, greatness is genius in undertakings of much pith and moment.
A clever or ingenious man is one who can do any thing
well, whether it is worth doing or not: a great man is
one who can do that which when done is of the highest
importance. Themistocles said he could not play on the
flute, but that he could make of a small city a great one.
This gives one a pretty good idea of the distinction in
question.

Greatness is great power, producing great effects. It is
not enough that a man has great power in himself, he
must shew it to all the world in a way that cannot be hid
or gainsaid. He must fill up a certain idea in the public
mind. I have no other notion of greatness than this
two-fold definition, great results springing from great
inherent energy. The great in visible objects has relation
to that which extends over space: the great in mental
ones has to do with space and time. No man is truly
great, who is great only in his life-time. The test of
greatness is the page of history. Nothing can be said to
be great that has a distinct limit, or that borders on
something evidently greater than itself. Besides, what is
short-lived and pampered into mere notoriety, is of a
gross and vulgar quality in itself. A Lord Mayor is hardly
a great man. A city orator or patriot of the day only
shew, by reaching the height of their wishes, the distance
they are at from any true ambition. Popularity is neither
fame nor greatness. A king (as such) is not a great man.
He has great power, but it is not his own. He merely
wields the lever of the state, which a child, an idiot, or a
madman can do. It is the office, not the man we gaze at.

Any one else in the same situation would be just as much an object of abject curiosity. We laugh at the country girl who having seen a king expressed her disappointment by saying, 'Why, he is only a man!' Yet, knowing this, we run to see a king as if he was something more than a man. – To display the greatest powers, unless they are applied to great purposes, makes nothing for the character of greatness. To throw a barleycorn through the eye of a needle, to multiply nine figures by nine in the memory, argues infinite dexterity of body and capacity of mind, but nothing comes of either. There is a surprising power at work, but the effects are not proportionate, or such as take hold of the imagination. To impress the idea of power on others, they must be made in some way to feel it. It must be communicated to their understandings in the shape of an increase of knowledge, or it must subdue and overawe them by subjecting their wills. Admiration, to be solid and lasting, must be founded on proofs from which we have no means of escaping; it is neither a slight nor a voluntary gift. A mathematician who solves a profound problem, a poet who creates an image of beauty in the mind that was not there before, imparts knowledge and power to others, in which his greatness and his fame consists, and on which it reposes. Jedediah Buxton will be forgotten; but Napier's bones will live. Lawgivers, philosophers, founders of religion, conquerors and heroes, inventors and great geniuses in arts and sciences, are great men; for they are great public benefactors, or formidable scourges to mankind. Among ourselves, Shakespear, Newton, Bacon, Milton, Cromwell, were great men; for they shewed great power by acts and thoughts, which have not yet been consigned to oblivion. They must needs be men of lofty stature, whose shadows lengthen out to remote posterity. A great farce-writer may be a great man; for Moliere was but a great farce-writer. In my mind, the author of Don Quixote was a great man. So have there been many others. A great chessplayer is not a great man, for he leaves the world as he found it. No act terminating in itself constitutes greatness. This will apply to all displays of power or trials of skill, which are confined to the momentary, individual effort, and construct no permanent image or trophy of themselves without them. Is not an actor then a great man, because 'he dies and leaves the world no copy?' I must make an exception for Mrs Siddons, or else give up my definition of greatness for her sake. A man at the top of his profession is not therefore a great man. He is great in his way, but that is all, unless he shews the marks of a great moving intellect, so that we trace the master-mind, and can sympathise with the springs that urge him on. The rest is but a craft or *mystery*. John Hunter was a great man – *that* any one might see without the smallest skill in surgery. His style and manner shewed the man. He would set about cutting up the carcase of a whale with the same greatness of *gusto* that Michael Angelo would have hewn a block of marble. Lord Nelson was a great naval commander; but for myself, I have not much opinion of a sea-faring life. Sir Humphry Davy is a great chemist, but I am not sure that he is a great man. I am not a bit the wiser for any of his discoveries, nor I never met with any one that was. But it is in the nature of greatness to propagate an idea of itself, as wave impels wave, circle without circle. It is a contradiction in terms for a coxcomb to be a great man. A really great man has always an idea of something greater than himself. I have observed that certain sectaries and polemical writers have no higher compliment to pay their most shining lights than to say that 'Such a one was a considerable man in his day.' Some new elucidation of a text sets aside the authority of the old interpretation, and a 'great scholar's memory outlives him half a century,' at the utmost. A rich man is not a great man, except to his dependants and his steward. A lord is a great man in the idea we have of his ancestry, and probably of himself, if we know nothing of him but his title. I have heard a story of two bishops, one of whom said (speaking of St Peter's at Rome) that when he first entered it, he was rather awe-struck, but that as he walked up it, his mind seemed to swell and dilate with it, and at last to fill the whole building – the other said that as he saw more of it, he appeared to himself to grow less and less every step he took, and in the end to dwindle into nothing. This was in some respects a striking picture of a great and little mind – for greatness sympathises with greatness, and littleness shrinks into itself. The one might have become a Wolsey; the other was only fit to become a Mendicant Friar – or there might have been court-reasons for making him a bishop. The French have to me a character of littleness in all about them; but they have produced three great men that belong to every country, Moliere, Rabelais, and Montaigne.

To return from this digression, and conclude the

Essay. A singular instance of manual dexterity was shewn in the person of the late John Cavanagh, whom I have several times seen. His death was celebrated at the time in an article in the Examiner newspaper (Feb. 7, 1819), written apparently between jest and earnest: but as it is *pat* to our purpose, and falls in with my own way of considering such subjects, I shall here take leave to quote it.

'Died at his house in Burbage-street, St Giles's, John Cavanagh, the famous hand fives-player. When a person dies, who does any one thing better than any one else in the world, which so many others are trying to do well, it leaves a gap in society. It is not likely that any one will now see the game of fives played in its perfection for many years to come – for Cavanagh is dead, and has not left his peer behind him. It may be said that there are things of more importance than striking a ball against a wall – there are things indeed which make more noise and do as little good, such as making war and peace, making speeches and answering them, making verses and blotting them; making money and throwing it away. But the game of fives is what no one despises who has ever played at it. It is the finest exercise for the body, and the best relaxation for the mind. The Roman poet said that "Care mounted behind the horseman and stuck to his skirts." But this remark would not have applied to the fives-player. He who takes to playing at fives is twice young. He feels neither the past nor future "in the instant." Debts, taxes, "domestic reason, foreign levy, nothing can touch him further." He has no other wish, no other thought, from the moment the game begins,

but that of striking the ball, of placing it, of *making* it!
This Cavanagh was sure to do. Whenever he touched
the ball, there was an end of the chase. His eye was
certain, his hand fatal, his presence of mind complete.
He could do what he pleased, and he always knew
exactly what to do. He saw the whole game, and played
it; took instant advantage of his adversary's weakness,
and recovered balls, as if by a miracle and from sudden
thought, that every one gave for lost. He had equal
power and skill, quickness, and judgment. He could
either out-wit his antagonist by finesse, or beat him by
main strength. Sometimes, when he seemed preparing
to send the ball with the full swing of his arm, he would
by a slight turn of his wrist drop it within an inch of the
line. In general, the ball came from his hand, as if from
a racket, in a straight horizontal line; so that it was in
vain to attempt to overtake or stop it. As it was said of a
great orator that he never was at a loss for a word, and
for the properest word, so Cavanagh always could tell
the degree of force necessary to be given to a ball, and
the precise direction in which it should be sent. He did
his work with the greatest ease; never took more pains
than was necessary; and while others were fagging themselves to death, was as cool and collected as if he had
just entered the court. His style of play was as remarkable
as his power of execution. He had no affectation, no
trifling. He did not throw away the game to show off an
attitude, or try an experiment. He was a fine, sensible,
manly player, who did what he could, but that was more
than any one else could even affect to do. His blows
were not undecided and ineffectual – lumbering like

Mr Wordsworth's epic poetry, nor wavering like Mr Coleridge's lyric prose, nor short of the mark like Mr Brougham's speeches, nor wide of it like Mr Canning's wit, nor foul like the *Quarterly*, not *let* balls like the *Edinburgh Review*. Cobbett and Junius together would have made a Cavanagh. He was the best *up-hill* player in the world; even when his adversary was fourteen, he would play on the same or better, and as he never flung away the game through carelessness and conceit, he never gave it up through laziness or want of heart. The only peculiarity of his play was that he never *volleyed*, but let the balls hop; but if they rose an inch from the ground, he never missed having them. There was not only nobody equal, but nobody second to him. It is supposed that he could give any other player half the game, or beat him with his left hand. His service was tremendous. He once played Woodward and Meredith together (two of the best players in England) in the Fives-court, St Martin's-street, and made seven and twenty aces following by services alone – a thing unheard of. He another time played Peru, who was considered a first-rate fives-player, a match of the best out of five games, and in the first three games, which of course decided the match, Peru got only one ace. Cavanagh was an Irishman by birth, and a house-painter by profession. He had once laid aside his working-dress, and walked up, in his smartest clothes, to the Rosemary Branch to have an afternoon's pleasure. A person accosted him, and asked him if he would have a game. So they agreed to play for half-a-crown a game, and a bottle of cider. The first game began – it was seven, eight, ten, thirteen, fourteen, all. Cavanagh won it. The next was the same. They played on, and each game was hardly contested. "There," said the unconscious fives-player, "there was a stroke that Cavanagh could not take: I never played better in my life, and yet I can't win a game. I don't know how it is." However, they played on, Cavanagh winning every game, and the bystanders drinking the cider, and laughing all the time. In the twelfth game, when Cavanagh was only four, and the stranger thirteen, a person came in, and said, "What! are you here, Cavanagh?" The words were no sooner pronounced than the astonished player let the ball drop from his hand, and saying, "What! have I been breaking my heart all this time to beat Cavanagh?" refused to make another effort. "And yet, I give you my word," said Cavanagh, telling the story with some triumph, "I played all the while with my clenched fist." – He used frequently to play matches at Copenhagen-house for wagers and dinners. The wall against which they play is the same that supports the kitchen-chimney, and when the wall resounded louder than usual, the cooks exclaimed, "Those are the Irishman's balls," and the joints trembled on the spit! – Goldsmith consoled himself that there were places where he too was admired: and Cavanagh was the admiration of all the fives-courts, where he ever played. Mr Powell, when he played matches in the Court in St Martin's-street, used to fill his gallery at half a crown a head, with amateurs and admirers of talent in whatever department it is shown. He could not have shown himself in any ground in England, but he would have been immediately surrounded with inquisitive gazers, trying to find out in what part of his frame his unrivalled skill lay, as politicians wonder to see the balance of Europe suspended in Lord Castlereagh's face, and admire the trophies of the British Navy lurking under Mr Croker's hanging brow. Now Cavanagh was as good-looking a man as the Noble Lord, and much better looking than the Right Hon. Secretary. He had a clear, open countenance, and did not look sideways or down, like Mr Murray the bookseller. He was a young fellow of sense, humour, and courage. He once had a quarrel with a waterman at Hungerford-stairs, and, they say, served him out in great style. In a word, there are hundreds at this day, who cannot mention his name without admiration, as the best fives-player that perhaps ever lived (the greatest excellence of which they have any notion) – and the noisy shout of the ring happily stood him in stead of the unheard voice of posterity! – The only person who seems to have excelled as much in another way as Cavanagh did in his, was the late John Davies, the racket-player. It was remarked of him that he did not seem to follow the ball, but the ball seemed to follow him. Give him a foot of wall, and he was sure to make the ball. The four best racket-players of that day were Jack Spines, Jem Harding, Armitage, and Church. Davies could give any one of these two hands a time, that is, half the game, and each of these, at their best, could give the best player now in London the same odds. Such are the gradations in all exertions of human skill and art. He once played four capital players together, and beat them. He was also a first-rate tennis-player, and excellent fives-player. In the

Fleet or King's Bench, he would have stood against Powell, who was reckoned the best open-ground player of his time. This last-mentioned player is at present the keeper of the Fives-court, and we might recommend to him for a motto over his door – "Who enters here, forgets himself, his country, and his friends." And the best of it is, that by the calculation of the odds, none of the three are worth remembering! – Cavanagh died from the bursting of a blood-vessel, which prevented him from playing for the last two or three years. This, he was often heard to say, he thought hard upon him. He was fast recovering, however, when he was suddenly carried off, to the regret of all who knew him. As Mr Peel made it a qualification of the present Speaker, Mr Manners Sutton, that he was an excellent moral character, so Jack Cavanagh was a zealous Catholic, and could not be persuaded to eat meat on a Friday, the day on which he died. We have paid this willing tribute to his memory.

> "Let no rude hand deface it,
>   And his forlorn '*Hic Jacet*'*" '

From *Table-Talk* (1821).

---

* Here he lies.

On the Spirit of Monarchy

'Strip it of its externals, and what is it but *a jest?*'
Charade on the word MAJESTY.

'As for politics, I think poets are *Tories* by nature, supposing them to be by nature poets. The love of an individual person or family, that has worn a crown for many successions, is an inclination greatly adapted to the fanciful tribe. On the other hand, mathematicians, abstract reasoners, of no manner of attachment to persons, at least to the visible part of them, but prodigiously devoted to the ideas of virtue, liberty, and so forth, are generally *Whigs*. It happens agreeably enough to this maxim, that the Whigs are friends to that wise, plodding, unpoetical people, the Dutch.'

– *Shenstone's Letters*, 1746.

The Spirit of Monarchy, then, is nothing but the craving in the human mind after the Sensible and the One. It is not so much a matter of state necessity or policy, as a natural infirmity, a disease, a false appetite in the popular feeling, which must be gratified. Man is an individual animal with narrow faculties, but infinite desires, which he is anxious to concentrate in some one object within the grasp of his imagination, and where, if he cannot be all that he wishes himself, he may at least contemplate his own pride, vanity, and passions, displayed in their most extravagant dimensions in a being no bigger and no better than himself. Each individual would (were it in his power) be a king, a God: but as he cannot, the next best thing is to see this reflex image of his self-love, the darling passion of his breast, realized, embodied out of himself in the first object he can lay his hands on for the purpose. The slave admires the tyrant because the last *is*, what the first *would be*. He surveys himself all over in the glass of royalty. The swelling bloated, self-importance of the one is the very counter-part and ultimate goal of the abject servility of the other. But both hate mankind for the same reason, because a respect for humanity is a diversion to their inordinate self-love, and the idea of the general good is a check to the gross intemperance of passion. The worthlessness of the object does not diminish but irritate the propensity to admire. It serves to pamper our imagination equally, and does not provoke our envy. All we want is to aggrandize our own vain-glory at second hand; and the less of real superiority or excellence there is in the person we fix upon as our proxy in this dramatic exhibition, the more easily can we change places with him, and fancy ourselves as good as he. Nay, the descent favours the rise; and we heap our tribute of applause the higher, in proportion as it is a free gift. An idol is not the worse for being of coarse materials; a king should be a commonplace man. Otherwise, he is superior in his own nature, and not dependent on our bounty or caprice. Man is a poetical animal, and delights in fiction. We like to have scope for the exercise of our mere will. We make kings of men, and Gods of stocks and stones: we are not jealous of the creatures of our own hands. We only want a peg or loop to hang our idle fancies on, a puppet to dress up, a lay-figure to paint from. It is 'THING Ferdinand, and not KING Ferdinand', as it was wisely and wittily observed. We ask only for the stage effect; we do not go behind the scenes, or it would go hard with many of our prejudices! We see the symbols of Majesty, we enjoy the pomp, we crouch before the power, we walk in the procession, and make part of the pageant, and we say in our secret hearts, there is nothing but accident that prevents us from being at the head of it. There is something in the mock-sublimity of thrones, wonderfully congenial to the human mind. Every man feels that he could sit there; every man feels that he could look big there; every man feels that he could bow there; every man feels that he could play the monarch there. The transition is so easy, and so delightful! The imagination keeps pace with royal state,

> 'And by the vision splendid
> Is on its way attended'.

The Madman in Hogarth who fancies himself a king, is not a solitary instance of this species of hallucination. Almost every true and loyal subject holds such a barren sceptre in his hand; and the meanest of the rabble, as he runs by the monarch's side, has wit enough to think – 'There goes my *royal* self!' From the most absolute despot to the lowest slave there is but one step (no, not one) in point of real merit. As far as truth or reason is concerned, they might change situations to-morrow – nay, they constantly do so without the smallest loss or benefit to mankind! Tyranny, in a word, is a farce got up for the entertainment of poor human nature; and it might pass very well, if it did not so often turn into a tragedy.

We once heard a celebrated and elegant historian and a hearty Whig declare, he liked a king like George III better than such a one as Buonaparte; because, in the former case, there was nothing to overawe the imagination but birth and situation; whereas he could not so easily brook the double superiority of the other, mental as well as adventitious. So does the spirit of independence and the levelling pride of intellect join in with the servile rage of the vulgar! This is the advantage which an hereditary has over an elective monarchy: for there is no end of the dispute about precedence while merit is supposed to determine it, each man laying claim to this in his own person; so that there is no other way to set aside all controversy and heart-burnings, but by precluding moral and intellectual qualifications altogether, and referring the choice to accident, and giving the preference to a nonentity. 'A good king', says Swift, 'should be, in all other respects, a mere cypher.'

It has been remarked, as a peculiarity in modern criticism, that the courtly and loyal make a point of crying up Mr Young, as an actor, and equally running down Mr Kean; and it has been conjectured in consequence that Mr Kean was a *radical*. Truly, he is not a radical politician; but what is as bad, he is a radical actor. He savours too much of the reality. He is not a mock-tragedian, an automaton player – he is something besides his paraphernalia. He has 'that within which passes show'. There is not a particle of affinity between him and the patrons of the court-writers. Mr Young, on the contrary, is the very thing – all assumption and strut and measured pomp, full of self-importance, void of truth and nature, the mask of the characters he takes, a pasteboard figure, a stiff piece of wax-work. He fills the throne of tragedy, not like an upstart or usurper, but as a matter of course, decked out in his plumes of feathers, and robes of state, stuck into a posture, and repeating certain words by rote. Mr Kean has a heart in his bosom, beating with human passion (a thing for the great 'to fear, not to delight in!'); he is a living man, and not an artificial one. How should those, who look to the surface, and never probe deeper, endure him? He is the antithesis of a court-actor. It is the object there to suppress and varnish over the feelings, not to give way to them. His *overt* manner must shock them, and be thought a breach of all decorum. They are in dread of his fiery humours, of coming near his Voltaic Battery – they choose rather to be roused gently from their self-complacent apathy by the application of Metallic Tractors. They dare not trust their delicate nerves within the estuary of the passions, but would slumber out their torpid existence in a calm, a Dead Sea – the air of which extinguishes life and motion!

Would it not be hard upon a little girl, who is busy in dressing up a favourite doll, to pull it in pieces before her face in order to show her the bits of wood, the wool, and rags it is composed of? So it would be hard upon that great baby, the world, to take any of its idols to pieces, and show that they are nothing but painted wood.

Neither of them would thank you, but consider the offer as an insult. The little girl knows as well as you do that her doll is a cheat; but she shuts her eyes to it, for she finds her account in keeping up the deception. Her doll is her pretty little self. In its glazed eyes, its cherry cheeks, its flaxen locks, its finery and its baby-house, she has a fairy vision of her own future charms, her future triumphs, a thousand hearts led captive, and an establishment for life. Harmless illusion! that can create something out of nothing, can make that which is good for nothing in itself so fine in appearance, and clothe a shapeless piece of deal-board with the attributes of a divinity! But the great world has been doing little else but playing at *make-believe* all its life-time. For several thousand years its chief rage was to paint larger pieces of wood and smear them with gore and call them Gods and offer victims to them – slaughtered hecatombs, the fat of goats and oxen, or human sacrifices – shewing in this its love of shew, of cruelty, and imposture; and woe to him who should 'peep through the blanket of the dark to cry, *Hold, hold*'. – *Great is Diana of the Ephesians*, was the answer in all ages. It was in vain to represent to them, 'Your Gods have eyes but they see not, ears but they hear not, neither do they understand' – the more stupid, brutish, helpless, and contemptible they were, the more furious, bigoted, and implacable were their votaries in their behalf.* The more absurd the fiction,

* 'Of whatsoe'er descent his Godhead be,
Stock, stone, or other homely pedigree,
In his defence his servants are as bold
As if he had been made of beaten gold.' – DRYDEN.

the louder was the noise made to hide it – the more mischievous its tendency, the more did it excite all the frenzy of the passions. Superstition nursed, with peculiar zeal, her rickety, deformed, and preposterous offspring. She passed by the nobler races of animals even, to pay divine honours to the odious and unclean – she took toads and serpents, cats, rats, dogs, crocodiles, goats and monkeys, and hugged them to her bosom, and dandled them into deities, and set up altars to them, and drenched the earth with tears and blood in their defence; and those who did not believe in them were cursed, and were forbidden the use of bread, of fire, and water, and to worship them was piety, and their images were held sacred, and their race became Gods in perpetuity and by divine right. To touch them, was sacrilege: to kill them, death, even in your own defence. If they stung you, you must die: if they infested the land with their numbers and their pollutions, there was no remedy. The nuisance was intolerable, impassive, immortal. Fear, religious horror, disgust, hatred, heightened the flame of bigotry and intolerance. There was nothing so odious or contemptible but it found a sanctuary in the more odious and contemptible perversity of human nature. The barbarous Gods of antiquity reigned *in contempt of their worshippers*!

This game was carried on through all the first ages of the world, and is still kept up in many parts of it; and it is impossible to describe the wars, massacres, horrors, miseries and crimes, to which it gave colour, sanctity, and sway. The idea of a God, beneficent and just, the invisible maker of all things, was abhorrent to their gross, material notions. No, they must have Gods of their own

making, that they could see and handle, that they knew to be nothing in themselves but senseless images, and these they daubed over with the gaudy emblems of their own pride and passions, and these they lauded to the skies, and grew fierce, obscene, frantic before them, as the representatives of their sordid ignorance and barbaric vices. TRUTH, GOOD, were idle names to them, without a meaning. They must have a lie, a palpable, pernicious lie, to pamper their crude, unhallowed conceptions with, and to exercise the untameable fierceness of their wills. The Jews were the only people of antiquity who were withheld from running headlong into this abomination; yet so strong was the propensity in them (from inherent frailty as well as neighbouring example) that it could only be curbed and kept back by the hands of Omnipotence.*
At length, reason prevailed over imagination so far, that these brute idols and their altars were overturned: it was thought too much to set up stocks and stones, Golden Calves and Brazen Serpents, as *bona fide* Gods and Goddesses, which men were to fall down and worship at their peril – and Pope long after summed up the merits of the whole mythologic tribe in a handsome distich –

> 'Gods partial, changeful, passionate, unjust,
>   Whose attributes were rage, revenge, or lust.'

It was thought a bold stride to divert the course of our imaginations, the overflowings of our enthusiasm, our

* They *would* have a king in spite of the devil. The image-worship of the Papists is a batch of the same leaven. The apishness of man's nature would not let even the Christian religion escape.

love of the mighty and the marvellous, from the dead to the living *subject*, and there we stick. We have got living idols, instead of dead ones; and we fancy that they are real, and put faith in them accordingly. Oh, Reason! when will thy long minority expire? It is not now the fashion to make Gods of wood and stone and brass, but we make kings of common men, and are proud of our own handy-work. We take a child from his birth, and we agree, when he grows up to be a man, to heap the highest honours of the state upon him, and to pay the most devoted homage to his will. Is there any thing in the person, 'any mark, any likelihood', to warrant this sovereign awe and dread? No: he may be little better than an idiot, little short of a madman, and yet he is no less qualified for king. If he can contrive to pass the College of Physicians, the Heralds' College dub him divine. Can we make any given individual taller or stronger or wiser than other men, or different in any respect from what nature intended him to be? No; but we can make a king of him. We cannot add a cubit to the stature, or instil a virtue into the minds of monarchs – but we can put a sceptre into their hands, a crown upon their heads, we can set them on an eminence, we can surround them with circumstance, we can aggrand-ize them with power, we can pamper their appetites, we can pander to their wills. We can do every thing to exalt them in external rank and station – nothing to lift them one step higher in the scale of moral or intellectual excellence. Education does not give capacity or temper; and the education of kings is not especially directed to useful knowledge or liberal sentiment. What then is the state of the case? The highest respect of the community and of every individual in it is paid and is due of right there, where perhaps not an idea can take root, or a single virtue be engrafted. Is not this to erect a standard of esteem directly opposite to that of mind and morals? The lawful monarch may be the best or the worst man in his dominions, he may be the wisest or the weakest, the wittiest or the stupidest: still he is equally entitled to our homage as king, for it is the place and power we bow to, and not the man. He may be a sublimation of all the vices and diseases of the human heart; yet we are not to say so, we dare not even think so. 'Fear God, and honour the King', is equally a maxim at all times and seasons. The personal character of the king has nothing to do with the question. Thus the extrinsic is set up over the intrinsic by authority: wealth and interest lend their countenance to gilded vice and infamy on principle, and outward show and advantages become the symbols and the standard of respect in despite of useful qualities or well-directed efforts through all ranks and gradations of society. 'From the crown of the head to the sole of the foot there is no soundness left.' The whole style of moral thinking, feeling, acting, is in a false tone – is hollow, spurious, meretricious. Virtue, says Montesquieu, is the principle of republics; honour, of a monarchy. But it is 'honour dishonourable, sin-bred' – it is the honour of trucking a principle for a place, of exchanging our honest convictions for a ribbon or a garter. The business of life is a scramble for unmerited precedence. Is not the highest respect entailed, the highest station filled without any possible proofs or pretensions to public spirit or public principle? Shall not the next places to it be secured by the sacrifice of them? It is the order of the day, the understood etiquette of courts and kingdoms. For the servants of the crown to presume on merit, when the crown itself is held as an heir-loom by prescription, is a kind of *lèse majesté*, an indirect attainder of the title to the succession. Are not all eyes turned to the sun of court-favour? Who would not then reflect its smile by the performance of any acts which can avail in the eye of the great, and by the surrender of any virtue, which attracts neither notice nor applause? The stream of corruption begins at the fountainhead of court-influence. The sympathy of mankind is that on which all strong feeling and opinion floats; and this sets in full in every absolute monarchy to the side of tinsel show and iron-handed power, in contempt and defiance of right and wrong. The right and the wrong are of little consequence, compared to the *in* and the *out*. The distinction between Whig and Tory is merely nominal: neither have their country one bit at heart. Phaw! we had forgot – Our British monarchy is a mixed, and the only perfect form of government; and therefore what is here said cannot properly apply to it. But MIGHT BEFORE RIGHT is the motto blazoned on the front of unimpaired and undivided Sovereignty!

A court is the centre of fashion; and no less so, for being the sink of luxury and vice –

– 'Of outward shew
Elaborate, of inward less exact'.

The goods of fortune, the baits of power, the indulgences of vanity, may be accumulated without end, and the taste for them increases as it is gratified: the love of virtue, the pursuit of truth, grow stale and dull in the dissipation of a court. Virtue is thought crabbed and morose, knowledge pedantic, while every sense is pampered, and every folly tolerated. Every thing tends naturally to personal aggrandizement and unrestrained self-will. It is easier for monarchs as well as other men 'to tread the primrose path of dalliance' than 'to scale the steep and thorny road to heaven'. The vices, when they have leave from power and authority, go greater lengths than the virtues; example justifies almost every excess, and 'nice customs curtsy to great kings'. What chance is there that monarchs should not yield to the temptations of gallantry then, when youth and beauty are as wax? What female heart can indeed withstand the attractions of a throne – the smile that melts all hearts, the air that awes rebellion, the frown that kings dread, the hand that scatters fairy wealth, that bestows titles, places, honour, power, the breast on which the star glitters, the head circled with a diadem, whose dress dazzles with its richness and its taste, who has nations at his command, senates at his control, 'in form and motion so express and admirable, in action how like an angel, in apprehension how like a God; the beauty of the world, the paragon of animals'! The power of resistance is so much the less, where fashion extends impunity to the frail offender, and screens the loss of character.

'Vice is undone, if she forgets her birth,
And stoops from angels to the dregs of earth;
But 'tis the fall degrades her to a whore:
Let greatness own her, and she's mean no more.
Her birth, her beauty, crowds and courts confess,
Chaste matrons praise her, and grave bishops bless.
In golden chains the willing world she draws,
And hers the Gospel is, and hers the laws.'*

The air of a court is not assuredly that which is most favourable to the practice of self-denial and strict moral-

---

* A lady of quality abroad, in allusion to the gallantries of the reigning Prince, being told, 'I suppose it will be your turn next?' said, 'No, I hope not; for you know it is impossible to refuse!' What a satire on the court and fashionables! If this be true, female virtue in the blaze of royalty is no more than the moth in the candle, or ice in the sun's ray. What will the great themselves say to it, in whom at that rate,

> – 'the same luck holds,
> They all are subjects, courtiers, and cuckolds!'

Out upon it! We'll not believe it. Alas! poor virtue, what is to become of the very idea of it, if we are to be told that every man within the precincts of a palace is an *hypothetical* cuckold, or holds his wife's virtue in trust for the Prince? We entertain no doubt that many ladies of quality have resisted the importunities of a throne, and that many more would do so in private life, if they had the desired opportunity: nay, we have been assured by several that a king would no more be able to prevail with them than any other man! If however there is any foundation for the above insinuation, it throws no small light on the Spirit of Monarchy, which by the supposition implies in it the *virtual* surrender of the whole sex at discretion; and at the same time accounts perhaps for the indifference shown by some monarchs in availing themselves of so mechanical a privilege.

ity. We increase the temptations of wealth, of power, and pleasure a thousand-fold, while we can give no additional force to the antagonist principles of reason, disinterested integrity and goodness of heart. Is it to be wondered at that courts and palaces have produced so many monsters of avarice, cruelty, and lust? The adept in voluptuousness is not likely to be a proportionable proficient in humanity. To feed on plate or be clothed in purple, is not to feel for the hungry and the naked. He who has the greatest power put into his hands, will only become more impatient of any restraint in the use of it. To have the welfare and the lives of millions placed at our disposal, is a sort of warrant, a challenge to squander them without mercy. An arbitrary monarch set over the heads of his fellows does not identify himself with them, or learn to comprehend their rights or sympathize with their interests, but looks down upon them as of a different species from himself, as insects crawling on the face of the earth, that he may trample on at his pleasure, or if he spares them, it is an act of royal grace; – he is besotted with power, blinded with prerogative, an alien to his nature, a traitor to his trust, and instead of being the organ of public feeling and public opinion, is an excrescence and an anomaly in the state, a bloated mass of morbid humours and proud flesh! A constitutional king, on the other hand, is a servant of the public, a representative of the people's wants and wishes, dispensing justice and mercy according to law. Such a monarch is the King of England! Such was his late, and such is his present Majesty George the IVth! –

Let us take the Spirit of Monarchy in its highest state

of exaltation, in the moment of its proudest triumph – a
Coronation-day. We now see it in our mind's eye; the
preparation of weeks – the expectation of months – the
seats, the privileged places, are occupied in the obscurity
of night, and in silence – the day dawns slowly, big with
the hope of Cæsar and of Rome – the golden censers are
set in order, the tables groan with splendour and with
luxury – within the inner space the rows of peeresses are
set, and revealed to the eye decked out in ostrich feathers
and pearls, like beds of lilies sparkling with a thousand
dew-drops – the marshals and the heralds are in motion
– the full organ, majestic, peals forth the Coronation
Anthem – every thing is ready – and all at once the
Majesty of kingdoms bursts upon the astonished sight –
his person is swelled out with all the gorgeousness of
dress, and swathed in bales of silk and golden tissues –
the bow with which he greets the assembled multitude,
and the representatives of foreign kings, is the climax of
conscious dignity, bending gracefully on its own bosom,
and instantly thrown back into the sightless air, as if
asking no recognition in return – the oath of mutual
fealty between him and his people is taken – the fairest
flowers of female beauty precede the Sovereign, scat-
tering roses; the sons of princes page his heels, holding
up the robes of crimson and ermine – he staggers and
reels under the weight of royal pomp, and of a nation's
eyes; and thus the pageant is launched into the open day,
dazzling the sun, whose beams seem beaten back by the
sun of royalty – there were the warrior, the statesman,
and the mitred head – there was Prince Leopold, like a
panther in its dark glossy pride, and Castlereagh, clad in

triumphant smiles and snowy satin, unstained with his own blood – the loud trumpet brays, the cannon roars, the spires are mad with music, the stones in the street are startled at the presence of a king: – the crowd press on, the metropolis heaves like a sea in restless motion, the air is thick with loyalty's quick pants in its monarch's arms – all eyes drink up the sight, all tongues reverberate the sound –

> 'A present deity they shout around,
> A present deity the vaulted roofs rebound!'

What does it all amount to? A show – a theatrical spectacle! What does it prove? That a king is crowned, that a king is dead! What is the moral to be drawn from it, that is likely to sink into the heart of a nation? That greatness consists in finery, and that supreme merit is the dower of birth and fortune! It is a form, a ceremony to which each successor to the throne is entitled in his turn as a matter of right. Does it depend on the inheritance of virtue, on the acquisition of knowledge in the new monarch, whether he shall be thus exalted in the eyes of the people? No: – to say so is not only an offence in manners, but a violation of the laws. The king reigns in contempt of any such pragmatical distinctions. They are set aside, proscribed, treasonable, as it relates to the august person of the monarch; what is likely to become of them in the minds of the people? A Coronation overlays and drowns all such considerations for a generation to come, and so far it serves its purpose well. It debauches the understandings of the people, and makes them the slaves of sense and show. It laughs to scorn and tramples upon every other claim to distinction or respect. Is the chief person in the pageant a tyrant? It does not lessen, but aggrandize him to the imagination. Is he the king of a free people? We make up in love and loyalty what we want in fear. Is he young? He borrows understanding and experience from the learning and tried wisdom of councils and parliaments. Is he old? He leans upon the youth and beauty that attend his triumph. Is he weak? Armies support him with their myriads. Is he diseased? What is health to a staff of physicians? Does he die? The truth is out, and he is then – nothing!

There is a cant among court-sycophants of calling all those who are opposed to them 'the *rabble*', '*fellows*', '*miscreants*', &c. This shows the grossness of their ideas of all true merit, and the false standard of rank and power by which they measure every thing; like footmen, who suppose their masters must be gentlemen, and that the rest of the world are low people. Whatever is opposed to power, they think despicable; whatever suffers oppression, they think deserves it. They are ever ready to side with the strong, to insult and trample on the weak. This is with us a pitiful fashion of thinking. They are not of the mind of Pope, who was so full of the opposite conviction, that he has even written a bad couplet to express it: –

'Worth makes the man, and want of it the fellow:
The rest is all but leather and prunella.'

Those lines in Cowper also must sound very puerile or old-fashioned to courtly ears: –

> 'The only amaranthine flower on earth
> Is virtue; the only lasting treasure, truth.'

To this sentiment, however, we subscribe our hearts and hands. There is nothing truly liberal but that which postpones its own claims to those of propriety – or great, but that which looks out of itself to others. All power is but an unabated nuisance, a barbarous assumption, an aggravated injustice, that is not directed to the common good: all grandeur that has not something corresponding to it in personal merit and heroic acts, is a deliberate burlesque, and an insult on common sense and human nature. That which is true, the understanding ratifies: that which is good, the heart owns: all other claims are spurious, vitiated, mischievous, false – fit only for those who are sunk below contempt, or raised above opinion. We hold in scorn all *right-lined* pretensions but those of rectitude. If there is offence in this, we are ready to abide by it. If there is shame, we take it to ourselves: and we hope and hold that the time will come, when all other idols but those which represent pure truth and real good, will be looked upon with the same feelings of pity and wonder that we now look back to the images of Thor and Woden!

Really, that men born to a throne (limited or unlimited) should employ the brief span of their existence here in doing all the mischief in their power, in levying cruel wars and undermining the liberties of the world, to prove to themselves and others that their pride and passions are of more consequence than the welfare of mankind at large, would seem a little astonishing, but that the fact is so. It is not our business to preach lectures to monarchs, but if we were at all disposed to attempt the ungracious task, we should do it in the words of an author who often addressed the ear of monarchs.

'A man may read a sermon,' says Jeremy Taylor, 'the best and most passionate that ever man preached, if he shall but enter into the sepulchres of kings. In the same Escorial where the Spanish princes live in greatness and power, and decree war or peace, they have wisely placed a cemetery where their ashes and their glory shall sleep till time shall be no more: and where *our* kings have been crowned, their ancestors lie interred, and they must walk over their grandsire's head to take his crown. There is an acre sown with royal seed, the copy of the greatest change from rich to naked, from ceiled roofs to arched coffins, from living like Gods to die like men. There is enough to cool the flames of lust, to abate the height of pride, to appease the itch of covetous desires, to sully and dash out the dissembling colours of a lustful, artificial, and imaginary beauty. There the warlike and the peaceful, the fortunate and the miserable, the beloved and the despised princes mingle their dust, and pay down their symbol of mortality, and tell all the world, that when we die our ashes shall be equal to kings, and our accounts shall be easier, and our pains for our crimes shall be less. To my apprehension, it is a sad record which is left by Athenæus concerning Ninus, the great Assyrian monarch, whose life and death is summed up in these words: "Ninus, the Assyrian, had an ocean of gold, and other riches more than the sand in the Caspian sea; he never saw the stars, and perhaps he never desired it; he never stirred up the holy fire among the Magi; nor touched his God with the sacred rod, according to the laws; he never offered sacrifice, nor worshipped the Deity, nor administered justice, nor spake to the people, nor numbered them; but he was most valiant to eat and drink, and having mingled his wines, he threw the rest upon the stones. This man is dead: behold his sepulchre, and now hear where Ninus is. *Sometime I was Ninus, and drew the breath of a living man, but now am nothing but clay. I have nothing but what I did eat, and what I served to myself in lust is all my portion: the wealth with which I was blest, my enemies meeting together shall carry away, as the mad Thyades carry a raw goat. I am gone to Hell; and when I went thither, I carried neither gold nor horse, nor a silver chariot. I that wore a mitre, am now a little heap of dust!"'* – Taylor's *Holy Living and Dying*.

From the *Liberal* for January 1823.
Not republished by Hazlitt.

What is the People?

March 7, 1818.

And who are you that ask the question? One of the people. And yet you would be something! Then you would not have the People nothing. For what is the People? Millions of men, like you, with hearts beating in their bosoms, with thoughts stirring in their minds, with the blood circulating in their veins, with wants and appetites, and passions and anxious cares, and busy purposes and affections for others and a respect for themselves, and a desire of happiness, and a right to freedom, and a will to be free. And yet you would tear out this mighty heart of a nation, and lay it bare and bleeding at the foot of despotism: you would slay the mind of a country to fill up the dreary aching void with the old, obscene, drivelling prejudices of superstition and tyranny: you would tread out the eye of Liberty (the light of nations) like 'a vile jelly', that mankind may be led about darkling to its endless drudgery, like the Hebrew Samson (shorn of his strength and blind), by his insulting taskmasters: you would make the throne every thing, and the people nothing, to be yourself less than nothing, a very slave, a reptile, a creeping, cringing sycophant, a court favourite, a pander to Legitimacy – that detestable fiction, which would make you and me and all mankind its slaves or victims; which would, of right and with all the sanctions of religion and morality, sacrifice the lives of millions to the least of its caprices; which subjects the rights, the happiness, and liberty of nations, to the will of some of the lowest of the species; which rears its bloated hideous form to brave the will of a whole people; that claims mankind as its property, and allows human nature to exist only upon sufferance; that haunts the understanding like a frightful spectre, and oppresses the very air with a weight that is not to be borne; that like a witch's spell covers the earth with a dim and envious mist, and makes us turn our eyes from the light of heaven, which we have no right to look at without its leave: robs us of 'the unbought grace of life', the pure delight and conscious pride in works of art or nature; leaves us no thought or feeling that we dare call our own; makes genius its lackey, and virtue its easy prey; sports with human happiness, and mocks at human misery; suspends the breath of liberty, and almost of life; exenterates us of our affections, blinds our understandings, debases our imaginations, converts the very hope of emancipation from its yoke into sacrilege, binds the successive countless generations of men together in its chains like a string of felons or galley-slaves, lest they should 'resemble the flies of a summer', considers any remission of its absolute claims as a gracious boon, an act of royal clemency and favour, and confounds all sense of justice, reason, truth, liberty, humanity, in one low servile deathlike dread of power without limit and without remorse!*

* This passage is nearly a repetition of what was said before; but as it contains the sum and substance of all I have ever said on such subjects, I have let it stand.

Such is the old doctrine of Divine Right, new-vamped up under the style and title of Legitimacy. 'Fine word, Legitimate!' We wonder where our English politicians picked it up. Is it an echo from the tomb of the martyred monarch, Charles the First? Or was it the last word which his son, James the Second, left behind him in his flight, and bequeathed with his *abdication*, to his legitimate successors? It is not written in our annals in the years 1688, in 1715, or 1745. It was not sterling then, which was only fifteen years before his present Majesty's accession to the throne. Has it become so since? Is the Revolution of 1688 at length acknowledged to be a blot in the family escutcheon of the Prince of Orange or the Elector of Hanover? Is the choice of the people, which raised them to the throne, found to be the only flaw in their title to the succession; the weight of royal gratitude growing more uneasy with the distance of the obligation? Is the alloy of liberty, mixed up with it, thought to debase that *fine carat*, which should compose the regal diadem? Are the fire-new specimens of the principles of the Right-Liners, and of Sir Robert Filmer's patriarchal scheme, to be met with in *The Courier, The Day, The Sun*, and some time back, in *The Times*, handed about to be admired in the highest circle, like the new gold coinage of sovereigns and half-sovereigns? We do not know. It may seem to be *Latter Lammas** with the doctrine at this time of day; but better late than never. By taking root in the soil of France, from which it was expelled (not quite so long as from our own), it may in time stretch out its feelers and

* A day that will never come.

strong suckers to this country; and present an altogether curious and novel aspect, by ingrafting the principles of the House of Stuart on the illustrious stock of the House of Brunswick.

'Miraturque novas frondes, et non sua poma.'*

What then is the People? We will answer first, by saying what it is not; and this we cannot do better than in the words of a certain author, whose testimony on the subject is too important not to avail ourselves of it again in this place. That infatuated drudge of despotism, who at one moment asks, 'Where is the madman that maintains the doctrine of divine right?' and the next affirms, that 'Louis XVIII has the same right to the throne of France, independently of his merits or conduct, that Mr Coke of Norfolk has to his estate at Holkham',† has given us a tolerable clue to what we have to expect from that mild paternal sway to which he would so kindly make us and the rest of the world over, in hopeless perpetuity. In a violent philippic against the author of the *Political Register*, he thus inadvertently expresses him-

* 'And [it] marvels at its new leaves and fruit not its own.'
† What is the amount of this right of Mr Coke's? It is not greater than that of the Lords Balmerino and Lovat to their estates in Scotland, or to the heads upon their shoulders, the one of which however were forfeited, and the other stuck upon Temple Bar, for maintaining, in theory and practice, that James II had the same right to the throne of these realms, independently of his merits or conduct, that Mr Coke has to his estate at Holkham. So thought they. So did not think George II.

self: – 'Mr Cobbett had been sentenced to two years' imprisonment for a libel, and during the time that he was in Newgate, it was discovered that he had been in treaty with Government to avoid the sentence passed upon him; and that he had proposed to certain of the agents of Ministers, that if they would let him off, they might make what future use they pleased of him; *he would entirely betray the cause of the people*; he would either write or not write, or *write against them*, as he had once done before, just as Ministers thought proper. To this, however, it was replied, that "Cobbett had written on too many sides already *to be worth a groat for the service of Government*"; and he accordingly suffered his confinement!' – We here then see plainly enough what it is that, in the opinion of this very competent judge, alone renders any writer 'worth a groat for the service of Government', *viz.* that he shall be able and willing entirely to betray the cause of the people. It follows from this principle (by which he seems to estimate the value of his lucubrations in the service of Government – we do not know whether the Government judge of them in the same way), that the cause of the people and the cause of the Government, who are represented as thus anxious to suborn their creatures to write against the people, are not the same but the reverse of one another. This slip of the pen in our professional retainer of legitimacy, though a libel on our own Government, is, notwithstanding, a general philosophic truth (the only one he ever hit upon), and an axiom in political mechanics, which we shall make the text of the following commentary.

What are the interests of the people? Not the interests

of those who would betray them. Who is to judge of those interests? Not those who would suborn others to betray them. That Government is instituted for the benefit of the governed, there can be little doubt; but the interests of the Government (when once it becomes absolute and independent of the people) must be directly at variance with those of the governed. The interests of the one are common and equal rights: of the other, exclusive and invidious privileges. The essence of the first is to be shared alike by all, and to benefit the community in proportion as they are spread: the essence of the last is to be destroyed by communication, and to subsist only – in wrong of the people. Rights and privileges are a contradiction in terms: for if one has more than his right, others must have less. The latter are the deadly nightshade of the commonwealth, near which no wholesome plant can thrive, – the ivy clinging round the trunk of the British oak, blighting its verdure, drying up its sap, and oppressing its stately growth. The insufficient checks and balances opposed to the overbearing influence of hereditary rank and power in our own Constitution, and in every Government which retains the least trace of freedom, are so many illustrations of this principle, if it needed any. The tendency in arbitrary power to encroach upon the liberties and comforts of the people, and to convert the public good into a stalking-horse to its own pride and avarice, has never (that we know) been denied by any one but 'the professional gentleman', who writes in *The Day* and *New Times*. The great and powerful, in order to be what they aspire to be, and what this gentleman would have them, perfectly independent of the will of the people, ought also to be perfectly independent of the assistance of the people. To be formally invested with the attributes of Gods upon earth, they ought first to be raised above its petty wants and appetites: they ought to give proofs of the beneficence and wisdom of Gods, before they can be trusted with the power. When we find them seated above the world, sympathizing with the welfare, but not feeling the passions of men, receiving neither good nor hurt, neither tilth nor tithe from them, but bestowing their benefits as free gifts on all, they may then be expected, but not till then, to rule over us like another Providence. We may make them a present of all the taxes they do not apply to their own use: they are perfectly welcome to all the power, to the possession of which they are perfectly indifferent, and to the abuse of which they can have no possible temptation. But Legitimate Governments (flatter them as we will) are not another Heathen mythology. They are neither so cheap nor so splendid as the Delphin edition of Ovid's *Metamorphoses*. They are indeed 'Gods to punish', but in other respects 'men of our infirmity'. They do not feed on ambrosia or drink nectar; but live on the common fruits of the earth, of which they get the largest share, and the best. The wine they drink is made of grapes: the blood they shed is that of their subjects: the laws they make are not against themselves: the taxes they vote, they afterwards devour. They have the same wants that we have: and having the option, very naturally help themselves first, out of the common stock, without thinking that others are to come after them. With the same natural necessities, they have a thousand artificial ones besides; and with a thousand times the means to gratify them, they are still voracious, importunate; unsatisfied. Our State-paupers have their hands in every man's dish, and fare sumptuously every day. They live in palaces, and loll in coaches. In spite of Mr Malthus, their studs of horses consume the produce of our fields, their dog-kennels are glutted with the food which would maintain the children of the poor. They cost us so much a year in dress and furniture, so much in stars and garters, blue ribbons, and grand crosses, – so much in dinners, breakfasts, and suppers, and so much in suppers, breakfasts, and dinners.* These heroes of the Income-tax, Worthies of the Civil List, Saints of the Court-calendar (*compagnons du lys*), have their naturals and non-naturals, like the rest of the world, but at a dearer rate. They are real *bona fide* personages, and do not live upon air. You will find it easier to keep them a week than a month; and at the end of that time, waking from the sweet dream of Legitimacy, you may say with Caliban, 'Why, what a fool was I to take this drunken monster for a God!' In fact, the case on the part of the people is so far self-evident. There is but a limited earth and a limited fertility to supply the demands both of Government and people; and what the one gains in the division of the spoil, beyond its average proportion, the other must needs go without. Do you suppose that our gentlemen-placemen and pensioners would suffer so many wretches to be perishing in our streets and highways, if they could relieve their extreme misery

* See the description of Gargantua in Rabelais.

without parting with any of their own superfluities? If the Government take a fourth of the produce of the poor man's labour, they will be rich, and he will be in want. If they can contrive to take one half of it by legal means, or by a stretch of arbitrary power, they will be just twice as rich, twice as insolent and tyrannical, and he will be twice as poor, twice as miserable and oppressed, in a mathematical ratio to the end of the chapter, that is, till the one can extort and the other endure no more. It is the same with respect to power. The will and passions of the great are not exerted in regulating the seasons, or rolling the planets round their orbits for our good, without fee or reward, but in controlling the will and passions of others, in making the follies and vices of mankind subservient to their own, and marring,

'Because men suffer it, their toy, the world'.

This is self-evident, like the former. Their will cannot be paramount, while any one in the community, or the whole community together, has the power to thwart it. A King cannot attain absolute power, while the people remain perfectly free; yet what King would not attain absolute power? While any trace of liberty is left among a people, ambitious Princes will never be easy, never at peace, never of sound mind; nor will they ever rest or leave one stone unturned, till they have succeeded in destroying the very name of liberty, or making it into a bye-word, and in rooting out the germs of every popular right and liberal principle from a soil once sacred to liberty. It is not enough that they have secured the whole power of the state in their hands, – that they carry every measure they please without the chance of an effectual opposition to it: but a word uttered against it is torture to their ears, – a thought that questions their wanton exercise of the royal prerogative rankles in their breasts like poison. Till all distinctions of right and wrong, liberty and slavery, happiness and misery, are looked upon as matters of indifference, or as saucy, insolent pretensions, – are sunk and merged in their idle caprice and pampered self-will, they will still feel themselves 'cribbed, confined, and cabin'd in': but if they can once more set up the doctrine of Legitimacy, 'the right divine of Kings to govern wrong', and set mankind at defiance with impunity, they will then be 'broad and casing as the general air, whole as the rock'. This is the point from which they set out, and to which by the grace of God and the help of man they may return again. Liberty is short and fleeting, a transient grace that lights upon the earth by stealth and at long intervals–

> 'Like the rainbow's lovely form,
> Evanishing amid the storm;
> Or like the Borealis race,
> That shift ere you can point their place;
> Or like the snow falls in the river,
> A moment white, then melts for ever'.

But power is eternal; it is 'enthroned in the hearts of Kings'. If you want the proofs, look at history, look at geography, look abroad; but do not look at home!

The power of an arbitrary King or an aspiring Minister

does not increase with the liberty of the subject, but must be circumscribed by it. It is aggrandized by perpetual, systematic, insidious, or violent encroachments on popular freedom and natural right, as the sea gains upon the land by swallowing it up. – What then can we expect from the mild paternal sway of absolute power, and its sleek minions? What the world has always received at its hands, an abuse of power as vexatious, cowardly, and unrelenting, as the power itself was unprincipled, preposterous, and unjust. They who get wealth and power from the people, who drive them like cattle to slaughter or to market, 'and levy cruel wars, wasting the earth', they who wallow in luxury, while the people are 'steeped in poverty to the very lips', and bowed to the earth with unremitting labour, can have but little sympathy with those whose loss of liberty and property is their gain. What is it that the wealth of thousands is composed of? The tears, the sweat, and blood of millions. What is it that constitutes the glory of the Sovereigns of the earth? To have millions of men their slaves. Wherever the Government does not emanate (as in our own excellent Constitution) from the people, the principle of the Government, the *esprit de corps*, the point of honour, in all those connected with it, and raised by it to privileges above the law and above humanity, will be hatred to the people. Kings who would be thought to reign in contempt of the people, will show their contempt of them in every act of their lives. Parliaments, not chosen by the people, will only be the instruments of Kings, who do not reign in the hearts of the people, 'to betray the cause of the people'. Ministers, not responsible to the people, will squeeze the last shilling out of them. *Charity begins at home*, is a maxim as true of Governments as of individuals. When the English Parliament insisted on its right of taxing the Americans without their consent, it was not from an apprehension that the Americans would, by being left to themselves, lay such heavy duties on their own produce and manufactures, as would afflict the generosity of the mother-country, and put the mild paternal sentiments of Lord North to the blush. If any future King of England should keep a wistful eye on the map of that country, it would rather be to hang it up as a trophy of legitimacy, and to 'punish the last successful example of a democratic rebellion', than from any yearnings of fatherly goodwill to the American people, or from finding his 'large heart' and capacity for good government, 'confined in too narrow room' in the united kingdoms of Great Britain, Ireland, and Hanover. If Ferdinand VII refuses the South American patriots leave to plant the olive or the vine, throughout that vast continent, it is his pride, not his humanity, that steels his royal resolution.*

In 1781, the Controller-general of France, under Louis XVI, Monsieur Joly de Fleury, defined the people of

---

* The Government of Ovando, a Spanish Grandee and Knight of Alcantara, who had been sent over to Mexico soon after its conquest, exceeded in treachery, cruelty, wanton bloodshed, and deliberate extortion, that of all those who had preceded him; and the complaints became so loud, that Queen Isabel on her death-bed requested that he might be recalled; but Ferdinand found that Ovando had sent home *much gold*, and he retained him in his situation. – See Capt. Burney's *History of the Buccaneers*.

France to be *un peuple serf, corvéable et baillable, à merci et miséricorde.** When Louis XVIII as the Count de Lille, protested against his brother's accepting the Constitution of 1792 (he has since become an accepter of Constitutions himself, if not an observer of them), as compromising the rights and privileges of the noblesse and clergy as well as of the crown, he was right in considering the Bastille, or 'King's castle', with the picturesque episode of the Man in the Iron Mask, the fifteen thousand *lettres de cachet*,† issued in the mild reign of Louis XV, *corvées*,‡ tithes, game-laws, holy water, the right of pillaging, imprisoning, massacring, persecuting, harassing, insulting, and ingeniously tormenting the minds and bodies of the whole French people at every moment of their lives, on every possible pretence, and without any check or control but their own mild paternal sentiments towards them, as among the *menus plaisirs*,¶ the chief points of etiquette, the immemorial privileges, and favourite amusements of Kings, Priests, and Nobles, from the beginning to the end of time, without which the bare title of King, Priest, or Noble, would not have been worth a groat.

The breasts of Kings and Courtiers then are not the safest depository of the interests of the people. But they know best what is for their good! Yes – to prevent it!

---

* A servile people, liable to forced labour and exploitation, at the mercy of others.
† Documents permitting members of the French nobility or ministry to imprison or deport a person without trial.
‡ Rent paid in labour.   ¶ Small pleasures.

The people may indeed feel their grievance, but their betters, it is said, must apply the remedy – which they take good care never to do! If the people want judgment in their own affairs (which is not certain, for they only meddle with their own affairs when they are forcibly brought home to them in a way which they can hardly misunderstand), this is at any rate better than the want of sincerity, which would constantly and systematically lead their superiors to betray those interests, from their having other ends of their own to serve. It is better to trust to ignorance than to malice – to run the risk of sometimes miscalculating the odds than to play against loaded dice. The people would in this way stand as little chance in defending their purses or their persons against Mr C— or Lord C—, as an honest country gentleman would have had in playing at put or hazard with Count Fathom or Jonathan Wild. A certain degree of folly, or rashness, or indecision, or even violence in attaining an object, is surely less to be dreaded than a malignant, deliberate, mercenary intention in others to deprive us of it. If the people must have attorneys, and the advice of counsel, let them have attorneys and counsel of their own choosing, not those who are employed by special retainer against them, or who regularly hire others *to betray their cause*.

> – 'O silly sheep,
>   Come ye to seek the lamb here of the wolf?'

This then is the cause of the people, the good of the people, judged of by common feeling and public opinion.

Mr Burke contemptuously defines the people to be 'any faction that at the time can get the power of the sword into its hands'. No: that may be a description of the Government, but it is not of the people. The people is the hand, heart, and head of the whole community acting to one purpose, and with a mutual and thorough consent. The hand of the people so employed to execute what the heart feels, and the head thinks, must be employed more beneficially for the cause of the people, than in executing any measures which the cold hearts, and contriving heads of any faction, with distinct privileges and interests, may dictate to betray their cause. The will of the people necessarily tends to the general good as its end; and it must attain that end, and can only attain it, in proportion as it is guided – First, by popular feeling, as arising out of the immediate wants and wishes of the great mass of the people, – secondly, by public opinion, as arising out of the impartial reason and enlightened intellect of the community. What is it that determines the opinion of any number of persons in things they actually feel in their practical and home results? Their common interest. What is it that determines their opinion in things of general inquiry, beyond their immediate experience or interest? Abstract reason. In matters of feeling and common sense, of which each individual is the best judge, the majority are in the right; in things requiring a greater strength of mind to comprehend them, the greatest power of understanding will prevail, if it has but fair play. These two, taken together, as the test of the practical measures or general principles of Government, must be right, cannot be wrong. It is an absurdity to suppose

that there can be any better criterion of national griev-
ances, or the proper remedies for them, than the aggregate amount of the actual, dear-bought experience, the
honest feelings, and heart-felt wishes of a whole people,
informed and directed by the greatest power of understanding in the community, unbiased by any sinister
motive. Any other standard of public good or ill must,
in proportion as it deviates from this, be vitiated in
principle, and fatal in its effects. *Vox populi vox Dei*,* is
the rule of all good Government: for in that voice, truly
collected and freely expressed (not when it is made the
servile echo of a corrupt Court, or a designing Minister),
we have all the sincerity and all the wisdom of the
community. If we could suppose society to be trans-
formed into one great animal (like Hobbes's *Leviathan*),
each member of which had an intimate connexion with
the head or Government, so that every want or intention
of every individual in it could be made known and
have its due weight, the State would have the same
consciousness of its own wants and feelings, and the
same interest in providing for them, as an individual has
with respect to his own welfare. Can any one doubt that
such a state of society in which the greatest knowledge
of its interests was thus combined with the greatest
sympathy with its wants, would realize the idea of a
perfect Commonwealth? But such a Government would
be the precise idea of a truly popular or *representative*
Government. The opposite extreme is the purely hereditary and despotic form of Government, where the people

* The voice of the people is the voice of God.

are an inert, torpid mass, without the power, scarcely with the will, to make its wants or wishes known: and where the feelings of those who are at the head of the State, centre in their own exclusive interests, pride, passions, prejudices; and all their thoughts are employed in defeating the happiness and undermining the liberties of a country.

Originally this, and 'What is the People (Concluded)' were published in three parts in the *Champion* for 12, 19 and 26 October 1817, then in two parts in the *Yellow Dwarf* for 7 and 14 March 1818. They were republished in *Political Essays, with Sketches of Public Characters* (1819).

On Reason and Imagination

I hate people who have no notion of any thing but generalities, and forms, and creeds, and naked propositions, even worse than I dislike those who cannot for the soul of them arrive at the comprehension of an abstract idea. There are those (even among philosophers) who, deeming that all truth is contained within certain outlines and common topics, if you proceed to add colour or relief from individuality, protest against the use of rhetoric as an illogical thing; and if you drop a hint of pleasure or pain as ever entering into 'this breathing world', raise a prodigious outcry against all appeals to the passions.

It is, I confess, strange to me that men who pretend to more than usual accuracy in distinguishing and analysing, should insist that in treating of human nature, of moral good and evil, the nominal differences are alone of any value, or that in describing the feelings and motives of men, any thing that conveys the smallest idea of what those feelings are in any given circumstances, or can by parity of reason ever be in any others, is a deliberate attempt at artifice and delusion – as if a knowledge or representation of things as they really exist (rules and definitions apart) was a proportionable departure from the truth. They stick to the table of contents, and never open the volume of the mind. They are for having maps, not pictures of the world we live in: as much as to say that a bird's-eye view of things contains the truth, the whole truth, and nothing but the truth. If you want to look for the situation of a particular spot, they turn to a pasteboard globe, on which they fix their wandering gaze; and because you cannot find the object of your search in their bald 'abridgements', tell you there is no such place, or that it is not worth inquiring after. They had better confine their studies to the celestial sphere and the signs of the zodiac; for there they will meet with no petty details to boggle at, or contradict their vague conclusions. Such persons would make excellent theologians, but are very indifferent philosophers. – To pursue this geographical reasoning a little farther. They may say that the map of a county or shire, for instance, is too large, and conveys a disproportionate idea of its relation to the whole. And we say that their map of the globe is too small, and conveys no idea of it at all.

> – 'In the world's volume
> Our Britain shows as of it, but not in it;
> In a great pool a swan's nest:'

but is it really so? What! the county is bigger than the map at any rate: the representation falls short of the reality, by a million degrees, and you would omit it altogether in order to arrive at a balance of power in the nonentities of the understanding, and call this keeping within the bounds of sense and reason; and whatever does not come within those self-made limits is to be set aside as frivolous or monstrous. But 'there are more things between heaven and earth than were ever dreamt of in this philosophy'. They cannot get them all in, *of the size of life*, and therefore they reduce them on a graduated scale, till they think they can. So be it, for certain necessary and general purposes, and in compliance with the infirmity of human intellect: but at other times, let us enlarge our conceptions to the dimensions of the original objects; nor let it be pretended that we have outraged truth and nature, because we have encroached on your diminutive mechanical standard. There is no language, no description that can strictly come up to the truth and force of reality: all we have to do is to guide our descriptions and conclusions by the reality. A certain proportion must be kept: we must not invert the rules of moral perspective. Logic should enrich and invigorate its decisions by the use of imagination; as rhetoric should be governed in its application, and guarded from abuse by the checks of the understanding. Neither, I apprehend, is sufficient alone. The mind can conceive only one or a few things in their integrity: if it proceeds to more, it must have recourse to artificial substitutes, and judge by comparison merely. In the former case, it may select the least worthy, and so distort the truth of things, by giving a hasty preference: in the latter, the danger is that it may refine and abstract so much as to attach no idea at all to them, corresponding with their practical value, or their influence on the minds of those concerned with them. Men act from individual impressions; and to know mankind, we should be acquainted with nature. Men act from passion; and we can only judge of passion by sympathy. Persons of the dry and husky class above spoken of, often seem to think even nature itself an interloper on their flimsy theories. They prefer the shadows in Plato's cave to the actual objects without it. They consider men 'as mice in an air-pump', fit only for their experiments; and do not consider the rest of the universe, or 'all the mighty world of eye and ear', as worth any notice at all. This is making short, but not sure work. Truth does not lie *in vacuo*, any more than in a well. We must improve our concrete experience of persons and things into the contemplation of general rules and principles; but without being grounded in individual facts and feelings, we shall end as we began, in ignorance.

It is mentioned in a short account of the *Last Moments of Mr Fox*, that the conversation at the house of Lord Holland (where he died) turning upon Mr Burke's style, that Noble Person objected to it as too gaudy and meretricious, and said that it was more profuse of flowers than fruit. On which Mr Fox observed, that though this was a common objection, it appeared to him altogether an unfounded one; that on the contrary, the flowers often concealed the fruit beneath them, and the ornaments of style were rather an hindrance than an advantage to the sentiments they were meant to set off. In confirmation of this remark, he offered to take down the book, and translate a page any where into his own plain, natural style; and by his doing so, Lord Holland was convinced that he had often missed the thought from having his attention drawn off to the dazzling imagery. Thus people continually find fault with the colours of style as incompatible with the truth of the reasoning, but without any

foundation whatever. If it were a question about the
figure of two triangles, and any person were to object
that one triangle was green and the other yellow, and
bring this to bear upon the acuteness or obtuseness of
the angles, it would be obvious to remark that the colour
had nothing to do with the question. But in a dispute
whether two objects are coloured alike, the discovery,
that one is green and the other yellow, is fatal. So with
respect to moral truth (as distinct from mathematical),
whether a thing is good or evil, depends on the quantity
of passion, of feeling, of pleasure and pain connected
with it, and with which we must be made acquainted in
order to come to a sound conclusion, and not on the
inquiry, whether it is round or square. Passion, in short,
is the essence, the chief ingredient in moral truth; and
the warmth of passion is sure to kindle the light of
imagination on the objects around it. The 'words that
glow' are almost inseparable from the 'thoughts that
burn'. Hence logical reason and practical truth are *dispar-
ates*. It is easy to raise an outcry against violent invectives,
to talk loud against extravagance and enthusiasm, to pick
a quarrel with every thing but the most calm, candid,
and qualified statement of facts: but there are enormities
to which no words can do adequate justice. Are we then,
in order to form a complete idea of them, to omit every
circumstance of aggravation, or to suppress every feeling
of impatience that arises out of the details, lest we should
be accused of giving way to the influence of prejudice
and passion? This would be to falsify the impression
altogether, to misconstrue reason, and fly in the face of
nature. Suppose, for instance, that in the discussions on

the Slave-Trade, a description to the life was given of the horrors of the *Middle Passage* (as it was termed), that you saw the manner in which thousands of wretches, year after year, were stowed together in the hold of a slave-ship, without air, without light, without food, without hope, so that what they suffered in reality was brought home to you in imagination, till you felt in sickness of heart as one of them, could it be said that this was a prejudging of the case, that your knowing the extent of the evil disqualified you from pronouncing sentence upon it, and that your disgust and abhorrence were the effects of a heated imagination? No. Those evils that inflame the imagination and make the heart sick, ought not to leave the head cool. This is the very test and measure of the degree of the enormity, that it involuntarily staggers and appals the mind. If it were a common iniquity, if it were slight and partial, or necessary, it would not have this effect; but it very properly carries away the feelings, and (if you will) overpowers the judgment, because it is a mass of evil so monstrous and unwarranted as not to be endured, even in thought. A man on the rack does not suffer the less, because the extremity of anguish takes away his command of feeling and attention to appearances. A pang inflicted on humanity is not the less real, because it stirs up sympathy in the breast of humanity. Would you tame down the glowing language of justifiable passion into that of cold indifference, of self-complacent, sceptical reasoning, and thus take out the sting of indignation from the mind of the spectator? Not, surely, till you have removed the nuisance by the levers that strong feeling alone can set at work, and have thus taken away the pang of suffering that caused it! Or say that the question were proposed to you, whether, on some occasion, you should thrust your hand into the flames, and were coolly told that you were not at all to consider the pain and anguish it might give you, nor suffer yourself to be led away by any such idle appeals to natural sensibility, but to refer the decision to some abstract, technical ground of propriety, would you not laugh in your adviser's face? Oh! no; where our own interests are concerned, or where we are sincere in our professions of regard, the pretended distinction between sound judgment and lively imagination is quickly done away with. But I would not wish a better or more philosophical standard of morality, than that we should think and feel towards others as we should, if it were our own case. If we look for a higher standard than this, we shall not find it; but shall lose the substance for the shadow! Again, suppose an extreme or individual instance is brought forward in any general question, as that of the cargo of sick slaves that were thrown overboard as so much *live lumber* by the captain of a Guinea vessel, in the year 1775, which was one of the things that first drew the attention of the public to this nefarious traffic,* or the practice of suspending contumacious negroes in cages to have their eyes pecked out, and to be devoured alive by birds of prey – Does this form no rule, because the mischief is solitary or excessive? The rule is absolute; for we feel that nothing of the kind could take place, or be tolerated for an instant, in any

---

* See *Memoirs of Granville Sharp*, by Prince Hoare, Esq.

system that was not rotten at the core. If such things are ever done in any circumstances with impunity, we know what must be done every day under the same sanction. It shows that there is an utter deadness to every principle of justice or feeling of humanity; and where this is the case, we may take out our tables of abstraction, and set down what is to follow through every gradation of petty, galling vexation, and wanton, unrelenting cruelty. A state of things, where a single instance of the kind can possibly happen without exciting general consternation, ought not to exist for half an hour. The parent, hydra-headed injustice ought to be crushed at once with all its viper brood. Practices, the mention of which makes the flesh creep, and that affront the light of day, ought to be put down the instant they are known, without inquiry and without repeal.

There was an example of eloquent moral reasoning connected with this subject, given in the work just referred to, which was not the less solid and profound, because it was produced by a burst of strong personal and momentary feeling. It is what follows: – 'The name of a person having been mentioned in the presence of Naimbanna (a young African chieftain), who was understood by him to have publicly asserted something very degrading to the general character of Africans, he broke out into violent and vindictive language. He was immediately reminded of the Christian duty of forgiving his enemies; upon which he answered nearly in the following words: – "If a man should rob me of my money, I can forgive him; if a man should shoot at me, or try to stab me, I can forgive him; if a man should sell me and all my family to a slave-ship, so that we should pass all the rest of our days in slavery in the West Indies, I can forgive him; but" (added he, rising from his seat with much emotion) "if a man takes away the character of the people of my country, I never can forgive him." Being asked why he would not extend his forgiveness to those who took away the character of the people of his country, he answered: "If a man should try to kill me, or should sell me and my family for slaves, he would do an injury to as many as he might kill or sell; but if any one takes away the character of Black people, that man injures Black people all over the world; and when he has once taken away their character, there is nothing which he may not do to Black people ever after. That man, for instance, will beat Black men, and say, *Oh, it is only a Black man, why should not I beat him?* That man will make slaves of Black people; for, when he has taken away their character, he will say, *Oh, they are only Black people, why should not I make them slaves?* That man will take away all the people of Africa if he can catch them; and if you ask him, But why do you take away all these people? he will say, *Oh! they are only Black people – they are not like White people – why should I not take them?* That is the reason why I cannot forgive the man who takes away the character of the people of my country."' – *Memoirs of Granville Sharp.*

I conceive more real light and vital heat is thrown into the argument by this struggle of natural feeling to relieve itself from the weight of a false and injurious imputation, than would be added to it by twenty volumes of tables and calculations of the *pros* and *cons* of right and wrong, of utility and inutility, in Mr Bentham's hand-writing. In allusion to this celebrated person's theory of morals, I will here go a step farther, and deny that the dry calculation of consequences is the sole and unqualified test of right and wrong; for we are to take into the account (as well) the reaction of these consequences upon the mind of the individual and the community. In morals, the cultivation of a *moral sense* is not the last thing to be attended to – nay, it is the first. Almost the only unsophisticated or spirited remark that we meet with in Paley's *Moral Philosophy*, is one which is also to be found in Tucker's *Light of Nature* – namely, that in dispensing charity to common beggars we are not to consider so much the good it may do the object of it, as the harm it will do the person who refuses it. A sense of compassion is involuntarily excited by the immediate appearance of distress, and a violence and injury is done to the kindly feelings by withholding the obvious relief, the trifling pittance in our power. This is a remark, I think, worthy of the ingenious and amiable author from whom Paley borrowed it. So with respect to the atrocities committed in the Slave-Trade, it could not be set up as a doubtful plea in their favour, that the actual and intolerable sufferings inflicted on the individuals were compensated by certain advantages in a commercial and political point of view – in a moral sense they *cannot* be compensated. They hurt the public mind: they harden and sear the natural feelings. The evil is monstrous and palpable; the pretended good is remote and contingent. In morals, as in philosophy, *De non apparentibus et non existentibus eadem est*

ratio.* What does not touch the heart, or come home to
the feelings, goes comparatively for little or nothing. A
benefit that exists merely in possibility, and is judged of
only by the forced dictates of the understanding, is not
a set-off against an evil (say of equal magnitude in itself)
that strikes upon the senses, that haunts the imagination,
and lacerates the human heart. A spectacle of deliberate
cruelty, that shocks every one that sees and hears of it,
is not to be justified by any calculations of cold-blooded
self-interest – is not to be permitted in any case. It
is prejudged and self-condemned. Necessity has been
therefore justly called 'the tyrant's plea'. It is no better
with the mere doctrine of utility, which is the sophist's
plea. Thus, for example, an infinite number of lumps of
sugar put into Mr Bentham's artificial ethical scales
would never weigh against the pounds of human flesh,
or drops of human blood, that are sacrificed to produce
them. The taste of the former on the palate is evanescent;
but the others sit heavy on the soul. The one is an object
to the imagination: the others only to the understanding.
But man is an animal compounded both of imagination
and understanding; and, in treating of what is good
for man's nature, it is necessary to consider both. A
calculation of the mere ultimate advantages, without
regard to natural feelings and affections, may improve
the external face and physical comforts of society, but
will leave it heartless and worthless in itself. In a word,
the sympathy of the individual with the consequences
of his own act is to be attended to (no less than the

---

* That which is not seen must be treated as if it did not exist.

consequences themselves) in every sound system of morality; and this must be determined by certain natural laws of the human mind, and not by rules of logic or arithmetic.

The aspect of a moral question is to be judged of very much like the face of a country, by the projecting points, by what is striking and memorable, by that which leaves traces of itself behind, or 'casts its shadow before'. Millions of acres do not make a picture; nor the calculation of all the consequences in the world a sentiment. We must have some outstanding object for the mind, as well as the eye, to dwell on and recur to – something marked and decisive to give a tone and texture to the moral feelings. Not only is the attention thus roused and kept alive; but what is most important as to the principles of action, the desire of good or hatred of evil is powerfully excited. But all individual facts and history come under the head of what these people call *Imagination*. All full, true, and particular accounts they consider as romantic, ridiculous, vague, inflammatory. As a case in point, one of this school of thinkers declares that he was qualified to write a better History of India from having never been there than if he had, as the last might lead to local distinctions or party-prejudices; that is to say, that he could describe a country better at second-hand than from original observation, or that from having seen no one object, place, or person, he could do ampler justice to the whole. It might be maintained, much on the same principle, that an artist would paint a better likeness of a person after he was dead, from description or different sketches of the face, than from having seen the individual living man. On the contrary, I humbly conceive that the seeing half a dozen wandering Lascars in the streets of London gives one a better idea of the soul of India, that cradle of the world, and (as it were) garden of the sun, than all the charts, records, and statistical reports that can be sent over, even under the clerical administration of Mr Canning. *Ex uno omnes.** One Hindoo differs more from a citizen of London than he does from all other Hindoos; and by seeing the two first, man to man, you know comparatively and essentially what they are, nation to nation. By a very few specimens you fix the great leading differences, which are nearly the same throughout. Any one thing is a better representative of its kind, than all the words and definitions in the world can be. The sum total is indeed different from the particulars; but it is not easy to guess at any general result, without some previous induction of particulars and appeal to experience.

'What can we reason, but from what we know?'

Again, it is quite wrong, instead of the most striking illustrations of human nature, to single out the stalest and tritest, as if they were most authentic and infallible; not considering that from the extremes you may infer the means, but you cannot from the means infer the extremes in any case. It may be said that the extreme and individual cases may be retorted upon us: – I deny it, unless it be with truth. The imagination is an *associating*

* All from one.

principle; and has an instinctive perception when a thing belongs to a system, or is only an exception to it. For instance, the excesses committed by the victorious besiegers of a town do not attach to the nation committing them, but to the nature of that sort of warfare, and are common to both sides. They may be struck off the score of national prejudices. The cruelties exercised upon slaves, on the other hand, grow out of the relation between master and slave; and the mind intuitively revolts at them as such. The cant about the horrors of the French Revolution is mere cant – every body knows it to be so: each party would have retaliated upon the other: it was a civil war, like that for a disputed succession: the general principle of the right or wrong of the change remained untouched. Neither would these horrors have taken place, except from Prussian manifestos, and treachery within: there were none in the American, and have been none in the Spanish Revolution. The massacre of St Bartholomew arose out of the principles of that religion which exterminates with fire and sword, and keeps no faith with heretics. – If it be said that nicknames, party watch-words, bugbears, the cry of 'No Popery', &c. are continually played off upon the imagination with the most mischievous effect, I answer that most of these bugbears and terms of vulgar abuse have arisen out of abstruse speculation or barbarous prejudice, and have seldom had their root in real facts or natural feelings. Besides, are not general topics, rules, exceptions, endlessly bandied to and fro, and balanced one against the other by the most learned disputants? Have not three-fourths of all the wars, schisms, heart-burnings in the world begun on mere points of controversy? – There are two classes whom I have found given to this kind of reasoning against the use of our senses and feelings in what concerns human nature, *viz.* knaves and fools. The last do it, because they think their own shallow dogmas settle all questions best without any farther appeal; and the first do it, because they know that the refinements of the head are more easily got rid of than the suggestions of the heart, and that a strong sense of injustice, excited by a particular case in all its aggravations, tells more against them than all the distinctions of the jurists. Facts, concrete existences, are stubborn things, and are not so soon tampered with or turned about to any point we please, as mere names and abstractions. Of these last it may be said,

'A breath can *mar* them, as a breath has made':

and they are liable to be puffed away by every wind of doctrine, or baffled by every plea of convenience. I wonder that Rousseau gave in to this cant about the want of soundness in rhetorical and imaginative reasoning; and was so fond of this subject, as to make an abridgement of Plato's rhapsodies upon it, by which he was led to expel poets from his commonwealth. Thus two of the most flowery writers are those who have exacted the greatest severity of style from others. Rousseau was too ambitious of an exceedingly technical and scientific mode of reasoning, scarcely attainable in the mixed questions of human life, (as may be seen in his *Social Contract* – a work of great ability, but extreme formality of structure) and it is probable he was led into this error in seeking to overcome his too great warmth of natural temperament and a tendency to indulge merely the impulses of passion. Burke, who was a man of fine imagination, had the good sense (without any of this false modesty) to defend the moral uses of the imagination, and is himself one of the grossest instances of its abuse.

It is not merely the fashion among philosophers – the poets also have got into a way of scouting individuality as beneath the sublimity of their pretensions, and the universality of their genius. The philosophers have become mere logicians, and their rivals mere rhetoricians; for as these last must float on the surface, and are not allowed to be harsh and crabbed and recondite like the others, by leaving out the individual, they become common-place. They cannot reason, and they must declaim. Modern tragedy, in particular, is no longer like a vessel making the voyage of life, and tossed about by the winds and waves of passion, but is converted into a handsomely-constructed steam-boat, that is moved by the sole expansive power of words. Lord Byron has launched several of these ventures lately (if ventures they may be called) and may continue in the same strain as long as he pleases. We have not now a number of *dramatis personæ* affected by particular incidents and speaking according to their feelings, or as the occasion suggests, but each mounting the rostrum, and delivering his opinion on fate, fortune, and the entire consummation of things. The individual is not of sufficient importance to occupy his own thoughts or the thoughts of others. The poet fills his page with *grandes pensées*. He

covers the face of nature with the beauty of his sentiments and the brilliancy of his paradoxes. We have the
subtleties of the head, instead of the workings of the
heart, and possible justifications instead of the actual
motives of conduct. This all seems to proceed on a false
estimate of individual nature and the value of human life.
We have been so used to count by millions of late, that we
think the units that compose them nothing; and are so
prone to trace remote principles, that we neglect the
immediate results. As an instance of the opposite style of
dramatic dialogue, in which the persons speak for themselves, and to one another, I will give, by way of illustra-
tion, a passage from an old tragedy, in which a brother has
just caused his sister to be put to a violent death.

'BOSOLA. Fix your eye here.
FERDINAND. Constantly.
BOSOLA. Do you not weep?
   Other sins only speak; murther shrieks out:
   The element of water moistens the earth;
   But blood flies upwards, and bedews the heavens.
FERDINAND. Cover her face: mine eyes dazzle; she died young.
BOSOLA. I think not so: her infelicity
   Seem'd to have years too many.
FERDINAND. She and I were twins:
   And should I die this instant, I had lived
   Her time to a minute.'

DUCHESS OF MALFI, Act IV. Scene 2.

How fine is the constancy with which he first fixes his
eye on the dead body, with a forced courage, and then,

as his resolution wavers, how natural is his turning his face away, and the reflection that strikes him on her youth and beauty and untimely death, and the thought that they were twins, and his measuring his life by hers up to the present period, as if all that was to come of it were nothing! Now, I would fain ask whether there is not in this contemplation of the interval that separates the beginning from the end of life, of a life too so varied from good to ill, and of the pitiable termination of which the person speaking has been the wilful and guilty cause, enough to 'give the mind pause'? Is not that revelation as it were of the whole extent of our being which is made by the flashes of passion and stroke of calamity, a subject sufficiently staggering to have place in legitimate tragedy? Are not the struggles of the will with untoward events and the adverse passions of others as interesting and instructive in the representation as reflections on the mutability of fortune or inevitableness of destiny, or on the passions of men in general? The tragic Muse does not merely utter muffled sounds: but we see the paleness on the cheek, and the life-blood gushing from the heart! The interest we take in our own lives, in our successes or disappointments, and the *home* feelings that arise out of these, when well described, are the clearest and truest mirror in which we can see the image of human nature. For in this sense each man is a microcosm. What he is, the rest are – whatever his joys and sorrows are composed of, theirs are the same – no more, no less.

'One touch of nature makes the whole world kin.'

But it must be the genuine touch of nature, not the outward flourishes and varnish of art. The spouting, oracular, didactic figure of the poet no more answers to the living man, than the lay-figure of the painter does. We may well say to such a one,

> 'Thou hast no speculation in those eyes
> That thou dost glare with: thy bones are marrowless,
> Thy blood is cold'!

Man is (so to speak) an endless and infinitely varied repetition: and if we know what one man feels, we so far know what a thousand feel in the sanctuary of their being. Our feeling of general humanity is at once an aggregate of a thousand different truths, and it is also the same truth a thousand times told. As is our perception of this original truth, the root of our imagination, so will the force and richness of the general impression proceeding from it be. The boundary of our sympathy is a circle which enlarges itself according to its propulsion from the centre – the heart. If we are imbued with a deep sense of individual weal or woe, we shall be awe-struck at the idea of humanity in general. If we know little of it but its abstract and common properties, without their particular application, their force or degrees, we shall care just as little as we know either about the whole or the individuals. If we understand the texture and vital feeling, we then can fill up the outline, but we cannot supply the former from having the latter given. Moral and poetical truth is like expression in a picture – the one is not to be attained by smearing over a large canvas, nor the other by bestriding a vague topic. In such matters, the most pompous sciolists are accordingly found to be the greatest contemners of human life. But I defy any great tragic writer to despise that nature which he understands, or that heart which he has probed, with all its rich bleeding materials of joy and sorrow. The subject may not be a source of much triumph to him, from its alternate light and shade, but it can never become one of supercilious indifference. He must feel a strong reflex interest in it, corresponding to that which he has depicted in the characters of others. Indeed, the object and end of playing, 'both at the first and now, is to hold the mirror up to nature', to enable us to feel for others as for ourselves, or to embody a distinct interest out of ourselves by the force of imagination and passion. This is summed up in the wish of the poet –

'To feel what others are, and know myself a man'.

If it does not do this, it loses both its dignity and its proper use.

From *The Plain Speaker* (1826).

On the Pleasure of Hating

There is a spider crawling along the matted floor of the room where I sit (not the one which has been so well allegorized in the admirable *Lines to a Spider*, but another of the same edifying breed) – he runs with heedless, hurried haste, he hobbles awkwardly towards me, he stops – he sees the giant shadow before him, and, at a loss whether to retreat or proceed, meditates his huge foe – but as I do not start up and seize upon the straggling caitiff, as he would upon a hapless fly within his toils, he takes heart, and ventures on, with mingled cunning, impudence, and fear. As he passes me, I lift up the matting to assist his escape, am glad to get rid of the unwelcome intruder, and shudder at the recollection after he is gone. A child, a woman, a clown, or a moralist a century ago, would have crushed the little reptile to death – my philosophy has got beyond that – I bear the creature no ill-will, but still I hate the very sight of it. The spirit of malevolence survives the practical exertion of it. We learn to curb our will and keep our overt actions within the bounds of humanity, long before we can subdue our sentiments and imaginations to the same mild tone. We give up the external demonstration, the *brute* violence, but cannot part with the essence or principle of hostility. We do not tread upon the poor little animal in question (that seems barbarous and pitiful!) but we regard it with a sort of mystic horror and superstitious loathing. It will ask another hundred years of fine writing and hard thinking to cure us of the prejudice, and make us feel towards this ill-omened tribe with something of 'the milk of human kindness', instead of their own shyness and venom.

Nature seems (the more we look into it) made up of antipathies: without something to hate, we should lose the very spring of thought and action. Life would turn to a stagnant pool, were it not ruffled by the jarring interests, the unruly passions of men. The white streak in our own fortunes is brightened (or just rendered visible) by making all around it as dark as possible; so the rainbow paints its form upon the cloud. Is it pride? Is it envy? Is it the force of contrast? Is it weakness or malice? But so it is, that there is a secret affinity, a *hankering* after evil in the human mind, and that it takes a perverse, but a fortunate delight in mischief, since it is a never-failing source of satisfaction. Pure good soon grows insipid, wants variety and spirit. Pain is a bitter-sweet, which never surfeits. Love turns, with a little indulgence, to indifference or disgust: hatred alone is immortal. – Do we not see this principle at work every where? Animals torment and worry one another without mercy: children kill flies for sport: every one reads the accidents and offences in a newspaper, as the cream of the jest: a whole town runs to be present at a fire, and the spectator by no means exults to see it extinguished. It is better to have it so, but it diminishes the interest; and our feelings take part with our passions, rather than with our understandings. Men assemble in crowds, with eager enthusiasm, to witness a tragedy: but if there were an execution going forward in the next street, as Mr Burke observes, the theatre would be left empty. A strange cur in a village, an idiot, a crazy woman, are set upon and baited by the whole community. Public nuisances are in the nature of public benefits. How long did the Pope, the Bourbons, and the Inquisition keep the people of England in breath, and supply them with nicknames to vent their spleen upon! Had they done us any harm of late? No: but we have always a quantity of superfluous bile upon the stomach, and we wanted an object to let it out upon. How loth were we to give up our pious belief in ghosts and witches, because we liked to persecute the one, and frighten ourselves to death with the other! It is not the quality so much as the quantity of excitement that we are anxious about: we cannot bear a state of indifference and *ennui*: the mind seems to abhor a *vacuum* as much as ever matter was supposed to do. Even when the spirit of the age (that is, the progress of intellectual refinement, warring with our natural infirmities) no longer allows us to carry our vindictive and headstrong humours into effect, we try to revive them in description, and keep up the old bugbears, the phantoms of our terror and our hate, in imagination. We burn Guy Faux in effigy, and the hooting and buffeting and maltreating that poor tattered figure of rags and straw makes a festival in every village in England once a year. Protestants and Papists do not now burn one another at the stake: but we subscribe to new editions of *Fox's Book of Martyrs*; and the secret of the success of the *Scotch Novels* is much the same – they carry us back to the feuds, the heart-burnings, the havoc, the dismay, the wrongs and the revenge of a barbarous age and people – to the rooted prejudices and deadly animosities of sects and parties in politics and religion, and of contending chiefs and clans in war and intrigue. We feel the full force of the spirit of hatred with all of them in turn. As we read, we throw aside the trammels of civilization, the flimsy veil of humanity. 'Off, you lendings!' The wild beast resumes its sway within us, we feel like hunting-animals, and as the hound starts in his sleep and rushes on the chase in fancy, the heart rouses itself in its native lair, and utters a wild cry of joy, at being restored once more to freedom and lawless, unrestrained impulses. Every one has his full swing, or goes to the Devil his own way. Here are no Jeremy Bentham Panopticons, none of Mr Owen's impassable Parallelograms, (Rob Roy would have spurned and poured a thousand curses on them), no long calculations of self-interest – the will takes its instant way to its object; as the mountain-torrent flings itself over the precipice, the greatest possible good of each individual consists in doing all the mischief he can to his neighbour: that is charming, and finds a sure and sympathetic chord in every breast! So Mr Irving, the celebrated preacher, has rekindled the old, original, almost exploded hell-fire in the aisles of the Caledonian Chapel, as they introduce the real water of the New River at Sadler's Wells, to the delight and astonishment of his fair audience. *'Tis pretty, though a plague*, to sit and peep into the pit of Tophet, to play at *snap-dragon* with flames and brimstone (it gives a smart electrical shock, a lively fillip to delicate constitutions), and to see Mr Irving, like a huge Titan, looking as grim and swarthy as if he had to forge tortures for all the damned! What a strange being man is! Not content with doing all he can to vex and hurt his fellows here, 'upon this bank and shoal of time', where one would think there were heart-aches, pain, disappointment, anguish, tears, sighs, and groans enough, the bigoted maniac takes him to the top of the high peak of school divinity to hurl him down the yawning gulf of penal fire; his speculative malice asks eternity to wreak its infinite spite in, and calls on the Almighty to execute its relentless doom! The cannibals burn their enemies and eat them, in good-fellowship with one another: meek Christian divines cast those who differ from them but a hair's-breadth, body and soul, into hell-fire, for the glory of God and the good of his creatures! It is well that the power of such persons is not co-ordinate with their wills: indeed, it is from the sense of their weakness and inability to control the opinions of others, that they thus 'outdo termagant', and endeavour to frighten them into conformity by big words and monstrous denunciations.

The pleasure of hating, like a poisonous mineral, eats into the heart of religion, and turns it to rankling spleen and bigotry; it makes patriotism an excuse for carrying fire, pestilence, and famine into other lands: it leaves to virtue nothing but the spirit of censoriousness, and a narrow, jealous, inquisitorial watchfulness over the actions and motives of others. What have the different sects, creeds, doctrines in religion been but so many pretexts set up for men to wrangle, to quarrel, to tear one another in pieces about, like a target as a mark to shoot at? Does any one suppose that the love of country in an Englishman implies any friendly feeling or disposition to serve another, bearing the same name? No, it means only hatred to the French, or the inhabitants of any other country that we happen to be at war with for the time. Does the love of virtue denote any wish to discover or amend our own faults? No, but it atones for an obstinate adherence to our own vices by the most virulent intolerance to human frailties. This principle is of a most universal application. It extends to good as well as evil: if it makes us hate folly, it makes us no less dissatisfied with distinguished merit. If it inclines us to resent the wrongs of others, it impels us to be as impatient of their prosperity. We revenge injuries: we repay benefits with ingratitude. Even our strongest partialities and likings soon take this turn. 'That which was luscious as locusts, anon becomes bitter as coloquintida'; and love and friendship melt in their own fires. We hate old friends: we hate old books: we hate old opinions; and at last we come to hate ourselves.

I have observed that few of those, whom I have formerly known most intimate, continue on the same friendly footing, or combine the steadiness with the warmth of attachment. I have been acquainted with two or three knots of inseparable companions, who saw each other 'six days in the week', that have broken up and dispersed. I have quarrelled with almost all my old friends, (they might say this is owing to my bad temper, but) they have also quarrelled with one another. What is become of 'that set of whist-players', celebrated by ELIA in his notable *Epistle to Robert Southey, Esq.* (and now I think of it – that I myself have celebrated in this very volume) 'that for so many years called Admiral Burney friend'? They are scattered, like last year's snow. Some of them are dead – or gone to live at a distance – or pass one another in the street like strangers; or if they stop to speak, do it as coolly and try to *cut* one another as soon as possible. Some of us have grown rich – others poor. Some have got places under Government – others a *niche* in the *Quarterly Review*. Some of us have dearly earned a name in the world; whilst others remain in their original privacy. We despise the one; and envy and are glad to mortify the other. Times are changed; we cannot revive our old feelings; and we avoid the sight and are uneasy in the presence of those, who remind us of our infirmity, and put us upon an effort at seeming cordiality, which embarrasses ourselves and does not impose upon our *quondam* associates. Old friendships are like meats served up repeatedly, cold, comfortless, and distasteful. The stomach turns against them. Either constant inter-course and familiarity breed weariness and contempt; or if we meet again after an interval of absence, we appear no longer the same. One is too wise, another too foolish for us; and we wonder we did not find this out before. We are disconcerted and kept in a state of continual alarm by the wit of one, or tired to death of the dullness of another. The *good things* of the first (besides leaving stings behind them) by repetition grow stale, and lose their startling effect; and the insipidity of the last becomes intolerable. The most amusing or instructive companion is at best like a favourite volume, that we wish after a time to *lay upon the shelf*; but as our friends are not willing to be laid there, this produces a misunderstanding and ill-blood between us. – Or if the zeal and integrity of friendship is not abated, or its career interrupted by any obstacle arising out of its own nature, we look out for other subjects of complaint and sources of dissatisfaction. We begin to criticize each other's dress, looks, and general character. 'Such a one is a pleasant fellow, but it is a pity he sits so late!' Another fails to keep his appointments, and that is a sore that never heals. We get acquainted with some fashionable young men or with a mistress, and wish to introduce our friend; but he is awkward and a sloven, the interview does not answer, and this throws cold water on our intercourse. Or he makes himself obnoxious to opinion – and we shrink from our own convictions on the subject as an excuse for not defending him. All or any of these causes mount up in time to a ground of coolness or irritation – and at last they break out into open violence as the only amends we can make ourselves for suppressing them so long, or the readiest means of banishing recollections of former kindness, so little compatible with our present feelings. We may try to tamper with the wounds or patch up the carcase of departed friendship, but the one will hardly bear the handling, and the other is not worth the trouble of embalming! The only way to be reconciled to old friends is to part with them for good: at a distance we may chance to be thrown back (in a waking dream) upon old times and old feelings: or at any rate, we should not think of renewing our intimacy, till we have fairly *spit our spite*, or said, thought, and felt all the ill we can of each other. Or if we can pick a quarrel with some one

ake him the scape-goat, this is an excellent
ce to heal a broken bone. I think I must be
s with Lamb again, since he has written that mag-
nimous *Letter to Southey*, and told him a piece of his
mind! – I don't know what it is that attaches me to H—
so much, except that he and I, whenever we meet, sit in
judgment on another set of old friends, and 'carve them
as a dish fit for the Gods'. There was L— H—, John Scott,
Mrs —, whose dark raven locks make a picturesque
background to our discourse, B—, who is grown fat, and
is, they say, married, R—; these had all separated long
ago, and their foibles are the common link that holds us
together. We do not affect to condole or whine over
their follies; we enjoy, we laugh at them till we are ready
to burst our sides, '*sans* intermission, for hours by the
dial'. We serve up a course of anecdotes, *traits*, master-
strokes of character, and cut and hack at them till we are
weary. Perhaps some of them are even with us. For my
own part, as I once said, I like a friend the better for
having faults that one can talk about. 'Then,' said Mrs —,
'you will never cease to be a philanthropist!' Those in
question were some of the choice-spirits of the age, not
'fellows of no mark or likelihood'; and we so far did
them justice: but it is well they did not hear what we
sometimes said of them. I care little what any one says
of me, particularly behind my back, and in the way of
critical and analytical discussion – it is looks of dislike
and scorn, that I answer with the worst venom of my
pen. The expression of the face wounds me more than
the expressions of the tongue. If I have in one instance
mistaken this expression, or resorted to this remedy

where I ought not, I am sorry for it. But the face was too fine over which it mantled, and I am too old to have misunderstood it! . . . I sometimes go up to —'s; and as often as I do, resolve never to go again. I do not find the old homely welcome. The ghost of friendship meets me at the door, and sits with me all dinner-time. They have got a set of fine notions and new acquaintance. Allusions to past occurrences are thought trivial, nor is it always safe to touch upon more general subjects. M. does not begin as he formerly did every five minutes, 'Fawcett used to say', &c. That topic is something worn. The girls are grown up, and have a thousand accomplishments. I perceive there is a jealousy on both sides. They think I give myself airs, and I fancy the same of them. Every time I am asked, 'If I do not think Mr Washington Irving a very fine writer?' I shall not go again till I receive an invitation for Christmas-day in company with Mr Liston. The only intimacy I never found to flinch or fade was a purely intellectual one. There was none of the cant of candour in it, none of the whine of mawkish sensibility. Our mutual acquaintance were considered merely as subjects of conversation and knowledge, not at all of affection. We regarded them no more in our experiments than 'mice in an air-pump': or like malefactors, they were regularly cut down and given over to the dissecting-knife. We spared neither friend nor foe. We sacrificed human infirmities at the shrine of truth. The skeletons of character might be seen, after the juice was extracted, dangling in the air like flies in cobwebs: or they were kept for future inspection in some refined acid. The demonstration was as beautiful as it was new. There is no surfeiting on gall: nothing keeps so well as a decoction of spleen. We grow tired of every thing but turning others into ridicule, and congratulating ourselves on their defects.

We take a dislike to our favourite books, after a time, for the same reason. We cannot read the same works for ever. Our honey-moon, even though we wed the Muse, must come to an end; and is followed by indifference, if not by disgust. There are some works, those indeed that produce the most striking effect at first by novelty and boldness of outline, that will not bear reading twice: others of a less extravagant character, and that excite and repay attention by a greater nicety of details, have hardly interest enough to keep alive our continued enthusiasm. The popularity of the most successful writers operates to wean us from them, by the cant and fuss that is made about them, by hearing their names everlastingly repeated, and by the number of ignorant and indiscriminate admirers they draw after them: – we as little like to have to drag others from their unmerited obscurity, lest we should be exposed to the charge of affectation and singularity of taste. There is nothing to be said respecting an author that all the world have made up their minds about: it is a thankless as well as hopeless task to recommend one that nobody has ever heard of. To cry up Shakespeare as the God of our idolatry, seems like a vulgar, national prejudice: to take down a volume of Chaucer, or Spenser, or Beaumont and Fletcher, or Ford, or Marlowe, has very much the look of pedantry and egotism. I confess it makes me hate the very name of Fame and Genius when works like these are 'gone into the wastes of time', while each successive generation of fools is busily employed in reading the trash of the day, and women of fashion gravely join with their waiting-maids in discussing the preference between *Paradise Lost* and Mr Moore's *Loves of the Angels*. I was pleased the other day on going into a shop to ask, 'If they had any of the *Scotch Novels*'? to be told – 'That they had just sent out the last, *Sir Andrew Wylie*!' – Mr Galt will also be pleased with this answer! The reputation of some books is raw and *unaired*: that of others is worm-eaten and mouldy. Why fix our affections on that which we cannot bring ourselves to have faith in, or which others have long ceased to trouble themselves about? I am half afraid to look into *Tom Jones*, lest it should not answer my expectations at this time of day; and if it did not, I should certainly be disposed to fling it into the fire, and never look into another novel while I lived. But surely, it may be said, there are some works, that, like nature, can never grow old; and that must always touch the imagination and passions alike! Or there are passages that seem as if we might brood over them all our lives, and not exhaust the sentiments of love and admiration they excite: they become favourites, and we are fond of them to a sort of dotage. Here is one:

> ' – Sitting in my window
> Printing my thoughts in lawn, I saw a God,
> I thought (but it was you), enter our gates;
> My blood flew out and back again, as fast
> As I had puffed it forth and sucked it in
> Like breath; then was I called away in haste

> To entertain you: never was a man
> Thrust from a sheepcote to a sceptre, raised
> So high in thoughts as I; you left a kiss
> Upon these lips then, which I mean to keep
> From you for ever. I did hear you talk
> Far above singing!'

A passage like this indeed leaves a taste on the palate like nectar, and we seem in reading it to sit with the Gods at their golden tables: but if we repeat it often in ordinary moods, it loses its flavour, becomes vapid, 'the wine of *poetry* is drank, and but the lees remain'. Or, on the other hand, if we call in the aid of extraordinary circumstances to set it off to advantage, as the reciting it to a friend, or after having our feelings excited by a long walk in some romantic situation, or while we

> ' – play with Amaryllis in the shade,
> Or with the tangles of Neæra's hair' –

we afterwards miss the accompanying circumstances, and instead of transferring the recollection of them to the favourable side, regret what we have lost, and strive in vain to bring back 'the irrevocable hour' – wondering in some instances how we survive it, and at the melancholy blank that is left behind! The pleasure rises to its height in some moment of calm solitude or intoxicating sympathy, declines ever after, and from the comparison and a conscious falling-off, leaves rather a sense of satiety and irksomeness behind it . . . 'Is it the same in pictures?' I confess it is, with all but those from Titian's hand. I don't know why, but an air breathes from his landscapes, pure, refreshing as if it came from other years; there is a look in his faces that never passes away. I saw one the other day. Amidst the heartless desolation and glittering finery of Fonthill, there is a portfolio of the Dresden Gallery. It opens, and a young female head looks from it; a child, yet woman grown; with an air of rustic innocence and the graces of a princess, her eyes like those of doves, the lips about to open, a smile of pleasure dimpling the whole face, the jewels sparkling in her crisped hair, her youthful shape compressed in a rich antique dress, as the bursting leaves contain the April buds! Why do I not call up this image of gentle sweetness, and place it as a perpetual barrier between mischance and me? – It is because pleasure asks a greater effort of the mind to support it than pain; and we turn, after a little idle dalliance, from what we love to what we hate!

As to my old opinions, I am heartily sick of them. I have reason, for they have deceived me sadly. I was taught to think, and I was willing to believe, that genius was not a bawd – that virtue was not a mask – that liberty was not a name – that love had its seat in the human heart. Now I would care little if these words were struck out of the dictionary, or if I had never heard them. They are become to my ears a mockery and a dream. Instead of patriots and friends of freedom, I see nothing but the tyrant and the slave, the people linked with kings to rivet on the chains of despotism and super-stition. I see folly join with knavery, and together make up public spirit and public opinions. I see the insolent Tory, the blind Reformer, the coward Whig! If mankind had wished for what is right, they might have had it long ago. The theory is plain enough; but they are prone to mischief, 'to every good work reprobate'. I have seen all that had been done by the mighty yearnings of the spirit and intellect of men, 'of whom the world was not worthy', and that promised a proud opening to truth and good through the vista of future years, undone by one man, with just glimmering of understanding enough to feel that he was a king, but not to comprehend how he could be king of a free people! I have seen this triumph celebrated by poets, the friends of my youth and the friends of man, but who were carried away by the infuriate tide that, setting in from a throne, bore down every distinction of right reason before it; and I have seen all those who did not join in applauding this insult and outrage on humanity proscribed, hunted down (they and their friends made a bye-word of), so that it has become an understood thing that no one can live by his talents or knowledge who is not ready to prostitute those talents and that knowledge to betray his species, and prey upon his fellow-man. 'This was some time a mystery: but the time gives evidence of it.' The echoes of liberty had awakened once more in Spain, and the morning of human hope dawned again: but that dawn has been overcast by the foul breath of bigotry, and those reviving sounds stifled by fresh cries from the time-rent towers of the Inquisition – man yielding (as it is fit he should) first to brute force, but more to the innate perversity and dastard spirit of his own nature, which leaves no room for farther hope or disappointment. And England, that arch-reformer, that heroic deliverer, that mouther about liberty and tool of power, stands gaping by, not feeling the blight and mildew coming over it, nor its very bones crack and turn to a paste under the grasp and circling folds of this new monster, Legitimacy! In private life do we not see hypocrisy, servility, selfishness, folly, and impudence succeed, while modesty shrinks from the encounter, and merit is trodden under foot? How often is 'the rose plucked from the forehead of a virtuous love to plant a blister there'! What chance is there of the success of real passion? What certainty of its continuance? Seeing all this as I do, and unravelling the web of human life into its various threads of meanness, spite, cowardice, want of feeling, and want of understanding, of indifference towards others and ignorance of ourselves – seeing custom prevail over all excellence, itself giving way to infamy – mistaken as I have been in my public and private hopes, calculating others from myself, and calculating wrong; always disappointed where I placed most reliance; the dupe of friendship, and the fool of love; have I not reason to hate and to despise myself? Indeed I do; and chiefly for not having hated and despised the world enough.*

From *The Plain Speaker* (1826).

* The only exception to the general drift of this Essay (and that is an exception in theory – I know of none in practice) is, that in reading we always take the right side, and make the case properly our own. Our imaginations are sufficiently excited, we have nothing to do with the matter but as a pure creation of the mind, and we therefore yield to the natural, unwarped impression of good and evil. Our own passions, interests, and prejudices out of the question, or in an

---

abstracted point of view, we judge fairly and conscientiously; for conscience is nothing but the abstract idea of right and wrong. But no sooner have we to act or suffer, than the spirit of contradiction or some other demon comes into play, and there is an end of common sense and reason. Even the very strength of the speculative faculty, or the desire to square things with an *ideal* standard of perfection (whether we can or no) leads perhaps to half the absurdities and miseries of mankind. We are hunting after what we cannot find, and quarrelling with the good within our reach. Among the thousands that have read *The Heart of Mid Lothian* there assuredly never was a single person who did not wish Jeanie Deans success. Even Gentle George was sorry for what he had done, when it was over, though he would have played the same prank the next day: and the *unknown* author, in his immediate character of contributor to *Blackwood* and the *Sentinel*, is about as respectable a personage as Daddy Ratton himself. On the stage, every one takes part with Othello against Iago. Do boys at school, in reading Homer, generally side with the Greeks or Trojans?